DARRÉN DAULTON

IF THEY ONLY KNEW

BLUE NOTE BOOKS
F L O R I D A

© Copyright 2008, Darren Daulton Enterprises

All rights reserved. No part of this book may be reproduced
or utilized in any form or by any means, electronic or
mechanical, including photocopying, recording, or by any
information storage and retrieval system, without written
permission from the publisher.

Published by Blue Note Books
1-800-624-0401

ISBN: 1-878398-93-8
ISBN 13: 978-1-878398-93-2

Library of Congress Control Number: 2007937342

www.darrendaulton.com

Cover design by: oddgraphic company; oddgraphic.com

Printed in the United States of America

Dedication

———————— • ————————

I would like to dedicate this book to all of the light workers who continue to do their jobs, regardless of the scrutiny they must endure.

Also, to the many people who are unaware of the different realities that exist in the same space and time as our third dimension.

Read this and the many more books written about this truth and believe…you will see these other dimensions when you start believing in them.

To Mom, Dad and Jr., I know you have had to deal with some unfortunate souls who "think" they know a lot and have written and said things that have broken your heart…You can relax now, "For the battle has been won!"

Last, but not least to my beautiful children: Zachary, Summer, Savannah and little Darren. I see a little Indigo in all of you and I cannot wait to share this information with you…in due time.

Acknowlegements

———————•———————

I would like to acknowledge all of the people who were brought together in divine order to get this book published.

Tony Perri, whose diligence and perseverance in forming and getting my company going and in making sure this book moved forward have been invaluable. Paul, Frankie and Kristin, who at Blue Note Books have helped me to take the important steps to become a published writer, and Laurie Hawkins, who has assisted in helping me to find the right words to tell my story.

Thank you to the other angels that have been put in my path to help facilitate all of this.

Most importantly, I thank the Lord our Creator, for revealing truth and reality to me.

There is nothing new under the sun, only our expanding consciousness. Truth and reality far exceed the religious endeavors of man's spiritual conquest.

I accept responsibility for my awakening to reveal these truths to the masses, in order to help change mass consciousness.

Foreword

———————— • ————————

I'M SUPPOSED TO WRITE A PARAGRAPH here for you to read that will grab your interest or entice you into picking this book up and adding it to your library. My first manuscript was roughly 500 pages and full of dirty laundry, so I decided against it. I thought I would scale it down to something short and to the point. The information in this book will be somewhat difficult to comprehend unless you have been awakened to the many other planes of existence that we live in, so I have written it in laymen's terms.

I grew up in a little town in Kansas dreaming of becoming a Major League Baseball player, just like many kids do. The cool thing was my dreams came true. For the last few years I have been telling friends and family that I was going to write a book. Everyone thought that was pretty neat as I was able to have an interesting baseball career that most sports fans would love to hear about. I was always a good leader and seemed to have the gift of knowing how things were or are supposed to work for the betterment of all. This has never left me regardless of what you might have heard or read about me.

The weird thing about this book is that it has absolutely nothing to do with my baseball career or most of my life for that matter. Granted, my life has been very interesting and very blessed. At the time of my retirement in 1998 I actually thought I had seen just about all this world has to offer and was going to ride off into the sunset and live happily ever after.

I was an All Star player, having played with and against the greatest players in the game and won a World Championship. I've met the greatest players in every sport, as well as actors, actresses, and Presidents. I have been in hurricanes, earthquakes, ran out of air while diving; nearly "checking out" a couple of times. You name it, I've done it.

Regardless of how all of this impacted my life, there were other things that started happening after I retired that quite frankly at the time were unexplainable. Now, they are very explainable and I want to share them with you. I really have no choice in this matter, as I know this was my ultimate calling as a leader.

I will save a lot of the stories for my website and will only share the ones that I feel will be beneficial to someone in need. The reason for this is that most people are very naïve about these phenomena and simply cannot digest them—not yet. I don't mean to offend anyone nor scare the hell out of them, however this information WILL help some people. What I write is all very real, but very difficult to convey as it was, and sometimes still is, very mind-boggling. Please relax and enjoy the challenge that follows.

1.

"For God Speaketh once, yea twice, yet man perceive it not.

In a dream, in a vision of the night, when deep sleep falleth upon men, in slumberings upon the bed;

Then he openeth the ears of men and sealeth their instruction,

That he may withdraw man from his purpose, and hide pride from man."

Job 33:14-17

Why Am I Writing This Book:
My Purpose

———————— • ————————

FOR THOSE OF YOU WHO DON'T KNOW ME, my name is Darren Daulton. There is really no difference between us other than I was gifted enough to play professional baseball for eighteen years. Fourteen of those years were in the Big Leagues with the Philadelphia Phillies and Florida Marlins.

One of the most memorable seasons was in 1993 with the Phillies. The country fell in love with that team. To this day, people are still talking about the cast of characters that went from worst to first in one season. I was traded to the Marlins down the stretch in 1997 and was able to help win a World Series. Primarily, my whole career was riddled with injuries, so my love-hate relationship with the game ended up with a ring and I was ready to retire.

After I left the game, negative things started happening in my life that one could not possibly try to do and have them all come true. There were things happening to me that seemed out of my control at the time. I will not bore you with the details as we all have baggage.

There was an incident that I went public with a while ago that resulted in some "goofs" having their day in the sun with it. I told about a time in 1997 when I was traded over to the Florida Marlins from the Phillies. We were playing in Wrigley Field against the Cubs and I hit a ball inside the 3rd base line to help us win the game. If you play 18 years professionally, fourteen of which are in the Big Leagues, you will have a damn good idea of what you can and cannot do. The crux of this story is: when I hit this particular ball inside the line, I felt as if someone else was swinging for me. I know that sounds weird, but you will have a much better understanding after reading this book. Let me explain the sensation I had at the time.

When I swung and hit the ball a feeling came over me that seemed very strange, like I was in another world although none of the surroundings changed. As I rounded first this feeling never left me. I felt like something divine had just occurred but I couldn't explain it at the time. I remember leaving the stadium and tears of joy or awe or whatever came over me. I had just experienced something beyond this world that we live in.

Talking about my Wrigley Field experience and metaphysics, along with countless media reports about my problems, brought a lot of attention. Over the last few years there has been much talk about what has happened to Dutch. Is he O.K.? The things he talks about are really out there. Has he lost his mind? Somebody said that he believes in aliens and that he enters into other dimensions. The guy is obviously on drugs or drinking way too much of Grand Pappy's cough syrup.

Trust me, if you are a close friend of mine I certainly have heard what you've said about me. Remember, when you are a celebrity, people love talking about you and people love telling the celebrity just who is in fact talking about them.

Not to worry, I haven't lost any sleep over it, but have always felt impelled to tell the world exactly what is going on and what I personally have experienced. I don't wish to share any of the issues that you might have read, heard or watched concerning my personal life. What I have to share is far more interesting than talking about people that have a difficult time getting along.

As for the experiences I was having, it got to the point where I wanted some answers. So I began to ask questions and do my own research. I wanted to dig really deep to find out what was going on. How did this happen? More importantly, it must mean that there is more to this life because I thought I had seen it all.

What I found is what I'm sharing with you in this book. What I found has changed my life and it answers questions about "what is going on" with me. I now know what happened to me in Wrigley Field and what explains the frequent experiences like it that have occurred.

Bear with me as there is so much to tell and I'm a baseball player, not a writer. I don't think of myself as an expert on these topics and I certainly don't have all the answers. There are many people who have experienced the same kinds of things for longer than I have and many others who can speak more eloquently to the theories and philosophies behind them. I didn't invent these theories; I am just living them.

I present these experiences and ideas to you not only to respond to my critics or answer some of the questions that people in the media have raised, but for you to consider and learn more. Maybe they will even explain some of your own experiences.

In order for you to open up your minds to the information in this book, you will need to do several things. First, suspend your beliefs if only for the short time you are here. If you are absolutely sure you have all the answers there is not much more I can say. Second, and I'll talk about this more in the next section, put aside your ego. Until you do, it will be the one factor that holds you back. If you take this step — putting aside your ego — you just might enjoy the read!

If your soul is spiritually ready and you really want the answers to life, then you will receive them. This won't happen until you are ready. I believe it to be a Universal Law that in Biblical terms you will be fed milk until you are able to digest the meat.

It's very easy to figure out who is ready and who isn't. The people that make derogatory comments about something they know nothing about are the very ones who aren't ready for the answers. This is plain and simple ignorance, no more, no less. These peoples' egos are still controlling their lives. There are young souls, middle-aged souls and old souls.

So here is my story. After writing and rewriting a manuscript with a lot of reluctance and procrastination, I now have something to share with you that I hope you can understand. I decided after writing those five hundred pages to get the crayons out and condense it to a short easy book that will introduce you to some fascinating concepts. Lord knows I could talk about this stuff for weeks on end because once you are awakened the information comes at you all day, every day.

One thing I have learned is we are easily programmed. Once something catches our attention, all that is required is that we be inundated with it. Eventually we HAVE to have it.

Critics and Ego

———————— • ————————

I WONDER WHAT IT WOULD BE LIKE to live your whole life as a critic. Can you imagine resting on your deathbed reflecting on your past accomplishments? *"Well, let's see, I spent my whole life trying to disprove everyone. I never really learned anything about myself because I was too busy showing others how wrong they were. I virtually lived my whole life saying wrong, never really enjoyed telling anyone they were right."* For crying out loud, they would have fired me and there are no jobs where they pay you to prove someone right.

In early 2006 I did a couple of interviews with the HBO television program, *Real Sports with Bryant Gumbel,* and the ESPN network about the subjects in this book. I'd always had a good relationship with the media when I was playing but I could never really understand why dirty laundry sold more than a good wholesome story in the society we live in. For some reason we consciously enjoy hearing negative things about other people. We feel better if Joe's life down the street is worse than ours. I believe it's because our EGOS are controlling our thoughts.

It is very interesting how people you don't even know and have never met before have the audacity to judge you, especially in a public forum. In all my travels I have never met TV reporter Bryant Gumbel, therefore I really don't perceive him as having the ability to judge me based on what his company formulated about me in a 12-minute piece. He is not alone. There are many other writers and media personalities that have judged me with no idea who I am.

One thing you must remember is that the media for the most part is trying their best to articulate something in a way that will provide the best opportunity to gain exposure. Not that there is anything wrong with that. Of course you want exposure and attention, that's your job. It's a fine line that is most certainly crossed. If roles were reversed, you certainly wouldn't want it happening to you or, more importantly, your wife or children.

Take all of these studs you see on television or hear on the radio that have never had their knuckles in the dirt, stood in a major league batters box, or tried to guard Michael Jordan. Do you really feel that these guys are qualified to give a correct reflection as to what is really going on down on the field at any particular moment or are they just giving another opinion? I believe it is the latter, as only experience can formulate a direct, correct analogy of what we are witnessing.

We have a propensity to judge others. Most certainly the act of judging others is derived from "being" judged at some point in time, which most likely left us feeling very uncomfortable. Had we never been judged, we most likely would never even know the ability to judge another. Such is life.

Don't get me wrong. I fully understand we have laws that require judgment in enforcing them. There is absolutely no good that will come out of talking about these episodes that could and should be left alone. You know it before you do it, but your ego ultimately wins out and you end up creating a mess. The funny thing about our society is that you will have people coming up to you telling you "nice job," very controversial. It is sad how the precedent has been set.

Now everyone knows your capabilities and the pressure is on, man. You've got a lot of attention, which is kind of cool. The big problem here is you've got to keep it up. You've got to judge everybody all the time now. This might not have been your initial intention, but by God it's paying the bills. You have created a monster that never reflects upon itself whether it's right, wrong or indifferent. The excuse now is "I'm giving them what they want!"

Hold on, it doesn't stop there. All of the other people in this occupation have witnessed this and voila, we have now created paparazzi. The beast in us has to be fed and there is no stopping us; "this is my job and I'm going to be better at it than the rest." There isn't a moral value whatsoever in this bowl of soup.

It's like the latest baseball scandal. If we can just prove that these guys are taking steroids, I guarantee I will sleep better, feel better and probably be able to make way more money for my family. This is absolutely going to change my life!

Give me a break folks, scenarios like this don't affect you one iota. It makes your over-inflated ego feel better because deep down you are not comfortable with you. That's the real reason you enjoy other people's misery. Do you really, really care? How much one way or another will YOU allow it to affect YOU and YOUR family?

If you aren't familiar with the term metaphysical, it means experiencing things above and beyond our five senses. In the physical world that we live in we have five senses that allow us to experience reality. Well, upon hearing my views most everyone got scared and tucked in their little furry tails, or their egos had to let the world know that I was out of my mind and very wrong. Ooooohhhhh! Sounds real scary to me!

Think about this. You can write an article of a miracle story in the Bible and have people read it without knowing it's from the Bible and then ask them if they believe it to be true. Their answer will be no, you cannot do that. Hand them a Bible and have them read the same story and ask them if they believe it to be true and most will say yes. Same story except people will believe what's written in the Bible because that's what they have been taught. They believe that the Bible is the inherent word of God and if he said it then it must be true. The paradox here is that God and this man named Jesus convey over and over in this book the powers and abilities that we all have within us, but when you tell someone of these wonderful phenomena that you are experiencing, people think you are crazy.

I suggested to you earlier to suspend your beliefs and put aside your ego to be open to what I'm writing here. You know, there is definitely something to this ego that drives us. I firmly believe that one never fully experiences life until he or she can live it being led by the heart and not the ego. I can certainly tell you that the other dimensions I speak of in this book cannot be experienced until you lay Mr. Ego aside.

Trust me on this; *he* will do everything in his power to remain at the helm of your ship.

If you choose to experience all of your divinity and learn to master all of your skills beyond your five senses, like Jesus, the hardest part will be dealing with your ego. Matter of fact when Mr. Ego is gone the rest of the fun just happens, whether you want it or not. That is called grace.

I hope you will read this book in its entirety and realize that there is much more to life than judging one another. I will share with you stories and information that I know for fact. I will also give you my opinion on things that I am unsure of; nevertheless the majority of you will definitely learn something.

So put aside your ego for a while. Trust me, *he* doesn't know as much as *he* thinks *he* does. I want to tap into your mind and hearts because there, and only there, will you be able to give and receive the correct information needed for this new world that is being created.

Ascension

———— • ————

THINGS ARE DEFINITELY CHANGING in the world we live in. The quagmire of this is 99.9% of the population really doesn't have a clue as to what these changes are, who they are or what they are capable of. Honestly, it wasn't long ago that I was one of that majority.

Open your mind and your heart and tuck in your ego. Here are the meat and potatoes of why I'm writing this book. I am talking about ASCENSION and being AWAKENED to the real world around you at all times. I am talking about my own awakening and what has happened to me.

Ascension is a spiritual journey. It is part of an evolutionary process of the universe that enables you to raise your level of consciousness higher and to tap into higher dimensions. It has been called a process of enlightenment where a person may escape the physical plane of existence. It is a time of mental and emotional clearing, of losing negative energies and continuing growth to reach and become a higher self.

What are the "dimensions" I refer to? The dimensions I talk about are states of consciousness, or also described as planes of existence. We have for as long as can be remembered lived in the 3rd dimension, or 3D, where we can see, feel, touch, taste and hear what exists. This 3rd dimension we live in is a physical dimension of matter that is recognized by us through our five senses. Everything you experience with your five senses is experienced as consciousness in the 3rd dimension.

Every dimension (also referred to as mansion or destiny) vibrates on a different frequency, just like different radio stations vibrate on different frequencies. In fact, all physical matter vibrates at a distinguishing frequency. In a nutshell, everything is a certain level of light. Everything. Everything made of matter is a level of light vibrating at a certain density. Bear with me, most of us are unaware of this because they're not exactly teaching it in our schools. It's not rocket science folks, it's just the majority of us have never been taught anything about ANY dimension for that matter. Why you haven't heard, I don't know other than your Bible says, "and you will know the truth and the truth will make you free." (John 8:32, Revised Standard Version)

Ascension is moving higher in consciousness, to the 4th dimension or the 5th dimension and even possibly beyond. Physical scientists have theorized that there could be ten or eleven dimensions. Metaphysics theory speaks of more. I'm not actually sure how many there are but I bet dollars to donuts there are 11 or 12. There are also lower sub planes as well as higher sub planes in each of these different dimensions.

The Fourth Dimension, also referred to as the astral plane, is associated with time. It is described as housing both the forces of light and darkness and in it are sourced magic, time travel and astral travel, karmic energy and reincarnation.[1] The Fifth Dimension is sometimes called the Plane of Light.

With my awakening I have experienced much in the 4th dimension and in the chapters that follow I'll give you some of the details. I believe, too, that I have been in the higher 5th dimension and that experience, too, will be included.

There are criteria that restrict from ascending; let's start with the basics. As I mentioned previously, the first thing that must go to enter into these other dimensions is your ego. Your desires and thoughts must start coming from your heart instead of your brain, which is most likely controlled by your ego. Once you start making your decisions through your heart you have opened yourself up to the mind of God. God is pure consciousness.

The Bible speaks of giving Him 10%… trust me it's not 10% of your pocket book. That's the biggest farce ever perpetrated on us who are so gullible. I don't believe God needs any more money so you can get to Heaven. (To me, that's kind of like car tollbooths and I know you like going through those.) He wants 10% of your mind and he will provide the spark that enables you to use the other 90%.

Once the ego is gone and you are heart-centered, your focus will shift to your physical bodies. You will need to study and understand your body and its energy. Releasing your body of the negative energy that has built up over eons is essential for ascending. The Chakras of the body, Kundalini energy and Mer-Ka-Ba are all part of your body energy and ascension and you'll learn more about them and other aspects later.

The people who are awakened know how energy works and how mass consciousness works. It is our job to inform the masses of what is taking place at this time in our history in hopes that people will stop thinking the way they do and realize the power we hold collectively. In short if everyone would start applying their heart instead of their ego, the condition of our society would change in the blink of an eye.

The paradox here is that until you are awakened you cannot experience it. Once you pierce the veil—metaphorically cross from the physical into the spiritual world - all of this will be revealed to you, so hold your tongue and it might save you from apologizing to me at a later date. When you understand all of this, you then start experiencing ascension and you will start taking on your light body that Jesus spoke of (White Robes). Don't get freaked out now and don't point your Doubting Thomas finger at me. I'm telling you the absolute truth and it will change your life forever.

Now will be a good time to grade yourself as to how far along your soul is in this grand game. There are many people who already know about the things I will share in this book and probably have written books themselves. The majority of people are still in the box and need that little nudge to help them get out of the box, even if we have the ones that don't care if there is a box as long as the bills are paid and the remote is resting firmly in hand.

Again, it's not rocket science, folks, we are just unaware. Not a big deal once you understand it, and believe me we have done it a billion times. To me this doesn't sound too dramatic. I actually understand this perfectly well, of course, as I'm an old soul. I know you can comprehend this stuff and hopefully something might jog your memory and you can start healing yourselves. Just believe!

2.

"*Wherefore, my beloved, as ye have always obeyed, not as in my presence only, but now much more in my absence, work out your own salvation with fear and trembling.*"

Philippians 2:12

What Is Happening and Why Isn't Everyone Aware?

———————•———————

ASCENSION IS NOT SOMETHING THAT I, alone, have experienced. What is happening is that the earth and all of its inhabitants are leaving the 3rd dimension, going through the 4th as we speak and headed to the 5th Dimension. Everything made of matter in the entire creation of the cosmos is experiencing ascension this very moment. Everything in creation has been through this many times and so have you. We all have experienced every one of these dimensions before "The Fall of Man." Once our mass consciousness changes we collectively can have our "Garden of Eden" back.

I do understand that most people really have no idea about this. I wish I had a figure as to how many people on the planet are aware of this but I haven't a clue—a growing number, as more people are being awakened every day. I wasn't aware until a few years ago. All of the awakened people reading this know exactly why I am conveying this in the manner I am because they also have had to deal with ignorance to the tenth degree. Don't get me wrong here;

we are very aware of the fact that most of the population isn't awakened yet. It is quite alright to be unaware of something but when you make an ego-based derogatory comment about something you don't know about, that's called plain and simple ignorance.

I don't mean to be redundant folks; it's just that I and a lot of other awakened people deal with this on a daily basis. I've got to tell you, the fact that you have been taught wrong for so long, you wouldn't know the truth if it was sitting on your lap. Better yet you have believed wrong for so long, you have no idea that truth is stranger than fiction. Read some of these articles that people write about when someone tells them something beyond their five senses. Primarily, the whole story is telling everyone how crazy this person is rather than using one's mind and trying to figure out how this could possibly happen. Interesting culture we live in!

What is also happening is cosmic cycles are aligning and we are coming to the end of this current dispensation of time. No, I didn't say it was the end of the world, as some will have you believe. I'm not sure what that really means. There was a man named Jesus that walked the earth two thousand years ago and yes they had ignorant people back then. Hardly anyone could understand what he was trying to teach them so their egos jailed him, hung him on a cross and killed him. Our ability to figure out what he was teaching hasn't changed much and now we are left with over twenty thousand religions. Jesus never taught religion, he taught spirituality.

Religion is man made; always has been and always will be. If you want to learn about religion you will be taught religion. If you want to learn about spirituality and the spirit realms, there is enough information and many brilliant people to teach it because they have witnessed them.

I will give you my opinion as to why some people are aware of what is happening and the majority are not. First of all, everybody is wired differently. Everyone is on their own time scale for their awakening. Remember the young souls, middle-aged souls and old souls. The people that are aware of what's going on not only sense it but also feel it in their physical bodies. I like to call these people sensitives, as they are very receptive to these influxes of energy that are bombarding us in these end of days. Your Bible calls it the Holy Spirit.

The Symptoms of Ascension

———————— • ————————

N OW THAT I'VE TOLD YOU ABOUT MY OWN awakening and that all of the inhabitants of the world are going through the process, you may be thinking: How would I know what to look for? What would I be experiencing?

There are a lot of physical symptoms that can occur during the ascension process, ranging from simple memory loss to feeling disoriented to feeling totally disconnected from the world as you once knew it. The list also includes feeling stress and intense energy, experiencing unusual physical pain, significant changes in sleep patterns, high and low emotional states and feeling a loss of identity from one's self. There are other symptoms that might be experienced as well.[2]

It's important to note that if you are having these symptoms, you should not be discouraged from seeing a medical doctor if you need one. They are discussed here for a reason so use your intuitive judgment when something arises. Remember, everyone is different and there are plenty of other symptoms that I might not cover in this book. For example, I experience intense head rushes sometimes when I stand up or stretch. I recall when I was younger experiencing head rushes but nothing near what I get now.

Each individual will experience ascension in their own way. Throughout the process, I wanted to share my experiences with someone but found nobody in my circle of friends that would understand. I found great information and support on the internet where I learned of others experiencing the same things. Hundreds of internet sites and books are devoted to the symptoms of ascension and the experiences of individuals and I'll provide a resource list on my website that you can use to learn more.

My own experiences reflect only my own awakening process — they are unique to me. But throughout them is a commonality with what the basic symptoms could be for all. I want to share them with you here.

Like many others who have experienced this process it has often been a difficult time for me. The physical and mental symptoms have created great stress. Everything I thought was reality was being questioned. This is the most horrible experience to go through, folks, because no human has ever consciously had to deal with this. Helping to guide people through it is a purpose of this book, in part due to the overwhelming feeling I have that getting this information out is, and has been, my ultimate destiny.

The feelings I had of disorientation were significant. Sometimes during a full moon, I literally felt as if I didn't belong in this world. I wondered where the one I knew went. While my surroundings looked familiar, I felt like I never belonged here.

I felt like I was living a different reality than what was actually physically happening. It was like thinking of something before it appeared. In fact, this is one of the symptoms I still feel quite often – even every day. The difference is when I first started ascending, I found this very bizarre especially because there was a lot of negativity going on in my life and I was manifesting negative things. The cool thing now is thinking of something and it manifesting positively.

I have noticed that parts of the old me are gone and I feel a loss of identity. I no longer care to entertain a lot of the things I used to do. Sometimes, if I can't spend time with my kids I really don't feel like doing anything.

This feeling of not belonging here and wanting out was very prevalent early on in my ascension. It was like wanting to go home. I didn't know what was happening and couldn't grasp the fact that the only life I ever knew, which by the way was a damn good one, was never coming back to me. At times I felt somewhat detached from my biological family as I was looking for a connection with my spiritual family. Depending on how far up Jacobs Ladder you have gone this might be difficult to understand.

My physical symptoms were numerous. I went through a period where my whole body felt like ants were crawling inside me. I experienced bowel disturbances — diarrhea or constipation or a combination of both. I had to pay close attention to what I consumed. I had symptoms of a cold or the flu, and my sleep was, and still is, often accompanied by night sweats and hot flashes.

The most frightening of all of these symptoms I faced were the respiratory problems—problems breathing, feeling out of breath and a rapid heart rate. I was always a guy who prided himself in being in tiptop shape. I had a couple experiences that felt like heart attacks that were scary enough to land my butt in the emergency room only to find out that I was perfectly healthy. I remember telling the doctor, "I understand what you are telling me, but I can't get any air." I was far enough along at the time and knew that this was part of the process, but it scared the hell out of me.

Obviously if you stay in somewhat good physical shape, the symptoms are not as drastic. In my research I found that millions of people are entering the emergency rooms around the globe for the same apparent reason.

Memory loss was often a problem for me and continues today. Like me, in your own ascension process there will be plenty of times that you will be in mid-sentence and completely forget what story you were trying to tell. I used to remember almost every pitch that was thrown throughout my career. At times I have trouble remembering last month.

I started out seeing unusual things, like lines on the floor. This would go on for quite some time. I am assuming these are grids like the same grids that are around every planet.[3] Then the grids seemed to flow into little specks of light that would be constantly flashing across my vision. If I sit comfortably in a chair and focus on the energy around me, I can start circling it at a very fast speed and certain things in my vision will disappear. I've always thought this was pretty cool.

Depending on your sensitivity you will most likely hear tones and ringing in your ears. There are different octaves as you ascend; there are lower octaves and higher octaves in the different dimensions. I try and take notice of what is going on while these tones are ringing just in case I am supposed to notice something.

I have also found that there are times when I am overly sensitive to stimuli that otherwise wouldn't have bothered me, like the noise of crowds and the sound of the television. I definitely go through these periods and can notice it in others.

Throughout the last few years of my conscious ascension I can tell physically that I go through periods of adjusting or acclimating. It's honestly like climbing Mt. Everest; you climb from camp to camp, staying at each period of time so your body can adjust. Usually when I start hearing the ringing in my ears it's time to move on. I will start to feel the intense energy flowing through me, normally the time when the hot sweats at night have arrived, meaning that my body is burning more density away. Full moons will kick your butt and after the intense energy leaves you, you will have trouble getting out of bed for a few days.

Periods of deep sleep were, and are, common for me as my

body rests and prepares for the new vibrational energy of a new phase. There are some mornings that I just cannot get out of bed regardless of how many hours I sleep. It seems the ascension process is like riding a roller coaster at times, having ups and downs. There is nothing better than being in the flow with everything around you, which is normally after one of these periods of not wanting to be active.

Ascension symptoms can also include increased psychic experiences and being able to perceive and experience other planes of existence, the other dimensions. I did. One thing you must realize if you are experiencing other dimensions or have psychic abilities such as telepathy, clairaudience, clairsentience, or clairvoyance is not to allow your ego to get in the way of why you have these gifts and others don't yet. Your job is to convey information about these gifts to others and let them know they too have these abilities, just as Jesus has told us. If they cannot understand this simple gesture of faith then they certainly aren't ready to tap the powers within themselves.

One of the difficult aspects of ascension is when old friends and things disappear and are not included in your awakening. This is not necessarily a negative thing, depending on circumstances, and one shouldn't feel bad because of a lesser desire to no longer hold the bond that was once had with a biological family. Jesus said we must be willing to let go of ALL our attachments in this world to experience the higher realms, you just might not have understood what the higher realms are. This loss of people can be difficult as you might not understand why all of this is happening in your life, but rest assured, it is part of the process and you will find your soul family members.

Maybe the most overriding of the symptoms is the feeling that you are going insane. What is happening may have you thinking that you are mentally ill. This can be very spooky until you acquire the ability to comprehend what is happening to you. You may want to speak with a professional counselor. I found that spending time in nature helped to keep me somewhat grounded.

As much as I hate to say this, feelings of anxiety and panic are going to happen during through this process. Anytime we are dealing with the EGO it is going to hurt. Sadly, I have read stories of people who just cannot handle these intense feelings. I know what I went through and trust me on this, if you experience what I did the people you expect to be able to help you through probably won't be any help at all. I promise you will feel like the world you used to live in is forever gone and the one you now live in is definitely not ideal. It will be harder if you are around negative, nagging or insecure people. Try to be around comforting, joyful people because it definitely helps.

The most important thing that I can convey to you in this book is the fact that you and only you are capable of finding yourself. Even though we ALL come from the same creator we experience 3D life as separate entities or souls. Once you figure out who you are in this game you are allowed to start ascending into the higher realms where you will realize that there is no separation and that we are all the same. Think back at times when you planned something but there was an overwhelming feeling that came over you and pulled you in another direction. This intuitive feeling is your soul, which IS YOU. Your soul has known everything you've done since creation and every thought and action that you've had is held in the etheric realm in what is called your akashic records.

For most of your life you have had the freedom of free will. It is my contention that we still do, except that times are changing and energy has to balance out for one to ascend, therefore we are helped in certain areas to stay out of these rut choices.

Hang in there and you can get through this. Remember first and foremost we are never given more than we can handle so suck it up and get through it. Fortunately, the gift of Mercy will allow you to reincarnate, a subject I discuss later on, but you will eventually have to experience this again. Why start over?

Finding your way to peace through this situation is the test you have set up for yourself. This is your journey and your soul would not have set it up if you weren't ready. YOU are the one who finds your way and you will. Looking back you will have gratitude for the experience and be a better person. I can assure you, though, that love, safety and unity will not be experienced until Mr. Ego takes a back seat. Fortunately for me, an overwhelming experience that I have had is to have a deep feeling of God's love. It has brought me to tears at times. For me this has been an overwhelming experience. If or when this happens you will believe that somehow, someway you were divinely picked by the hand of God.

The Physical
and the
Spritual Connection

———————•———————

A GREAT SHIFT IN CONSCIOUSNESS IS COMING. A new paradigm is approaching as the old ways of living and being are burning away. The old belief systems are leaving us. There is no doubt in my mind one or more events are happening that will completely alter your life: a death in the family, divorce, illness, a change in job status, loss of home or other catastrophe. "These are forces that cause you to slow down, simplify, change, re-examine who you are and what your life means to you. They are forces that you cannot ignore, forces that cause you to release your attachments, forces that awaken your senses of love and compassion." [4]

There is a combining of the spiritual world with the physical world. This is why people are experiencing changes in their physical bodies. The earth and other planets are experiencing the very same changes. Why do you see more destruction in nature at this point in our history? Check out all of the earthquakes, volcanoes, tornadoes and hurricanes, fires, floods and more that are happening around the globe. It's not just happening here on earth, it's on all of the planets. This is not a doom and gloom scenario, it's to inform you that everything of matter has to purge itself of density so it can take on more light to ascend into the higher realms. Don't shoot the messenger and remember that Jesus spoke all about this event.

Let me help you learn something here if you don't already know it and as I've said, there are many brilliant souls out there that can explain this stuff better than I. I can certainly help you when it comes to baseball, but quantum physics is something I consciously only learned about a couple of years ago.

Quantum physics is the study of things that are very small, that you cannot see with the naked eye. These are your protons, neutrons and electron particles; the building blocks of creation.

Here comes the learning part. Each of us has four bodies that I am aware of. If we have more, my research leaves me unaware. These four bodies are called our four lower bodies. We have a physical body that allows us to live in this current dimension that you and I and our egos agree on. We also have a spiritual body, an emotional body and a mental body. Our spiritual body is sometimes referred to as our etheric body.

I had no idea that we were spiritual beings with other etheric bodies. Our etheric bodies are provided for us to live in the etheric realms we cannot visually see unless we raise our frequency. Remember, Paul was shown these realms although he wasn't sure if he was in his physical body or not. Pretty bizarre statement wouldn't you agree? Once you are able to raise your frequency, you will fully understand what he is implying.

When all of our bodies are in sync, we experience pleasure — or ease — in our daily walk. When we have a disruption in one or more of our bodies, we feel dis-ease. Remember everything created is pure energy; everything is made up of these protons, neutrons and electrons.

Everything is constantly vibrating and there are all kinds of energy waves going through and around us at all times. We are being influenced by many different things. Obviously if you ingest the right things in your physical body it will have a major impact on your physical well-being. Once you are able to raise your level of consciousness, it will matter less what you put into your body. At the highest levels of consciousness, high enough where you can heal people, nothing you put into your body will harm it. You will realize that your mind is in control of everything. Very simple statement, folks; believe it. What about your other bodies though?

Your mental and emotional bodies are influenced by your mental and emotional well-being. We are spiritual beings that chose to come down to this lower density to experience this. We are spiritual first, please understand this. Most people believe they are human, living in a human body trying to become spiritual. This is a major hang up in not realizing your divinity and the power you already have. Make no mistake; you are a spiritual being, an alien to this planet, if you will. Your physical body was born here but your other bodies remain in the etheric realms, you cannot see them unless of course you are advanced enough in the ascension process.

If you are having a bad day, week, or month, you need to sit down with yourself and figure out just what is chapping your rear end. There is something influencing one or more of your bodies and something better change or you can ride this misery all the way 'til death.

I am not positive, but I believe dis-ease starts in our emotional and mental bodies and then ultimately ends up in our denser physical body. One thing I couldn't understand was when everyone was burying the actor Tom Cruise when he came out and said we have the ability to heal ourselves. Anyone who doesn't know this truth needs to join a book club. Don't blame your ignorance on a man who walks around everyday with a smile on his face loving life. If you're pissed because he is aware of something that you're not, my suggestion would be to pick his brain instead of ridiculing him. Maybe you will be able to walk around loving life with a smile on your face everyday. All you need to do is learn it. Again, you already know it, you just can't remember how to do it.

3.

"And that, knowing the time, that now it is high time to awake out of sleep: for now is our salvation nearer than when we believed."

Romans 13:11

The Energy of Awakening

———————— • ————————

THERE ARE IMPORTANT THINGS TO KNOW ABOUT the way the energies in and around our physical bodies are parts of the ascension process. Understanding this energy and the way it flows through our bodies is a fundamental part of our awakening. It must flow freely if we are to experience awakening and higher consciousness. As I have said, you must open your mind, let go of your ego and focus within. Then you can shift your attention to your physical body and really experience these forces.

I told you about dis-ease and the body and how our emotional states affect us. In the symptoms of ascension I explained how darkness and negative emotions were brought to consciousness, causing pain and difficulty in the process. These emotions had to happen because releasing your body of negative energy is a critical part of the ascension process. They had to be experienced again as they were released.

Where in our physical bodies are the keys to our personal energies? They are located in our spinal column, with the Chakras of the body and Kundalini energy. They are found in the pineal gland of our brain and even within our body's cells, in our DNA. And they are from the outside in the vibrational power of numbers or in the creation of Mer-Ka-Ba, our light bodies.

In the sections that follow I will tell you more about each of these in detail, explaining more about them and where they fit into ascension. Even though I am not a writer, this is kind of neat being able to tell others about these energies and what they can look forward to as they experience them. The only problem you will incur is reprogramming your minds into believing that you are capable of all of these phenomena. They are who you are and eventually you will remember. He finds all of his sheep and the most important one is the one that is lost.

Chakras

———— • ————

ALONG OUR SPINAL COLUMNS ARE SAID TO BE seven chakras, or energy centers of the body. These chakras rotate and allow us to receive and process energy that helps sustain us and keep us living healthy lives. Chakra is a Sanskrit word meaning wheel and chakras are said to be of a shape that is like a spinning disk. They are placed in seven different locations from the base of the spinal column to the head.

A chakra is not a physical element of the body that we can see but it is more of a spiritual "center" of energy and each of the seven chakras corresponds to a different aspect of our being such as self-knowledge, creativity, intuitive seeing and personal power.

There are also chakras outside of our bodies that are very much a part of our daily lives. We all have an aura around us. Some people have the ability to see these. I can see mine in certain light such as when the sun is rising. I don't have the ability to see colors in other peoples' auras but some people are very adept at this.

You may feel tingling all over as your chakras open allowing more energy to become unblocked and flow through your body. However, when you are angry or miserable you stop the flow of energy going through your bodies. If this continues most likely you will become sick or acquire some kind of a disease.

The people who can see auras can tell if you are miserable or not by the color and size of your aura. Go find one and ask them to read your aura. Disease is exactly what it reads, a dis–ease about something within ALL of your bodies. Do you believe our Creator would give us life but deny our ability to live it comfortably? Of course not; we have access to all of the answers but you have to change your beliefs and most everything you've been taught.

Ego reacts only to what it knows. Your mind however, when synchronizing with the mind of God, is never a constant; it is forever creating your future. Things cannot make you happy. Inner joy and satisfaction are what ultimately fill your appetite.

When we understand chakras, we begin to realize there is much more to us other than our physical bodies. We understand with these four lower bodies that I've written about that we need to have our chakras opened and receiving energy to maintain a healthy mind, body and soul.

Pineal Gland

———————— • ————————

W̲E̲ ̲A̲L̲S̲O̲ ̲H̲A̲V̲E̲ ̲W̲H̲A̲T̲ ̲I̲S̲ ̲C̲A̲L̲L̲E̲D̲ ̲A̲ ̲P̲I̲N̲E̲A̲L̲ ̲G̲L̲A̲N̲D̲, which is referred to as our "Third Eye." There is no doubt in my mind that most people haven't a clue what this is, where it's located or what it does. I have mentioned the pineal gland to a few people before and they looked at me as if I just turned purple. But many do know of this *mind's eye,* another name for it. Have you ever heard of the rock group "Third Eye Blind" who are said to have taken their name from this concept?

I will tell you later in the book how everything is connected but right now I will inform you that everything we are supposed to be awakening to in life is being brought to our attention. It is mass consciousness that changes our reality and simple gestures such as a band's name reach mass consciousness. These things happen every day, not because we try to do them, it's just the way energy works.

Back to the pineal gland. Since the time of the ancient Greeks, who believed this gland to be our connection to the realms of thought, the pineal gland has been the source of contemplation and inspiration. French philosopher, natural scientist and mathematician Renes Descartes (1596-1650) called it "the seat of the soul."[5] It is often associated with the sixth chakra, called the brow chakra, and some say it is the link between our physical and spiritual souls.

But what is the true purpose of this "Third Eye" in our physical bodies and our spiritual beings?

Unlike chakras and some of the other concepts in this book, the pineal gland is an actual part of our physical bodies and has a physiological function for us. Located deep in the brain, behind the eyes and the pituitary gland, this pea-sized gland secretes melatonin and is part of the body's internal timing system, or circadian rhythm.

It is because of the belief that the spiritual aspect of the pineal gland is dormant and can be activated to let us ascend to higher dimensions or to give us telepathic or psychic powers that I'm writing about it here. This activation can be by energies such as Kundalini – which I'll describe in the next section – or the meditation exercise which I discuss here.

We have the ability to activate our pineal gland and perceive these higher dimensions through a process that involves relaxation and mediation. It can happen when the exercise causes the pineal gland and pituitary body to vibrate in unison, creating a relationship that forms a magnetic field. The interaction of negative and positive forces creates what is also called the 'light in the head," which can support astral travel and other occult abilities. [6]

The process is not a difficult one. I have used it myself. You have to put yourself in a very relaxed mood and then concentrate on the spot between your eyes, staring at that point. This "point of realization" is located centrally between the middle of the forehead and the pineal gland. You want to visualize the subtle body escaping through the trap door of the brain, according to one writer, whereby "a popping sound may occur at the time of separation of the astral body in the area of the pineal gland."[7]

You will most likely start out seeing colors and shapes, very bright light, even numbers or what seem like codes. These beautiful shapes come into your view and then kind of fade out and then another one will come in. I am not sure why we see what we are seeing other than probably something that is supposed to jog our memory of who, and what, we are.

How about the pineal gland? Hope you got all that but there is plenty more. We all have the ability to activate our pineal glands and start experiencing other worlds.

Folks, I have to tell you this is an awesome experience. Of course, the first time I realized that I even had this thing that could take me into these other places I was a little freaked. Not scared, just surprised and very naïve as to this new awareness, and most importantly I wanted more of this, and now. I could see with my eyes closed!

There is only one time that I have ever heard the popping sound that I referenced. It's a little weird but nonetheless very real. It's kind of like popping the cork on a champagne bottle. I had already read about this popping sound before it happened to me, so as strange as it was I was very much aware of it. The people that are aware of this will corroborate how cool this is.

The more adept you are at seeing through your third eye, the more you are able to see and do. There have been times when I have actually seen other people in other dimensions while in this state, not to be confused with seeing people in other dimensions consciously with my eyes open. If you are able to do it once you will no doubt get the hang of it and understand how it works. Take a trip and never leave the farm!

When you activate the pineal gland you also have the ability to astral travel which I'll tell you about in the following sections. No doubt it's one of the coolest things I've ever done, other than time travel. Some people are very good at astral travel and can do it just about whenever they put their MIND to it, pun intended. I personally cannot do it whenever I want and trust me it's not from a lack of trying.

If and when you start experiencing these things you will absolutely change your priorities and engulf everything you can to find the answers to what you are experiencing. You are supposed to. It's your calling to WAKE UP! Everything happens in perfect divine order. Once you, metaphorically speaking, pick up your cross and follow, all of the answers will be given when you are ready.

Here is an interesting tidbit from the website Hiddenmeanings.com about the pineal gland of the brain and its relation to a Supernova found by scientists. Called Supernova 1987a, it was first seen in February 1987 and in 1997, when it was large enough, it was viewed with NASA's Hubble Space Telescope.[8] Bill Donahue, creator of hiddenmeanings.com, relates the science and spirituality of the Supernova, citing "ancient writings about a third eye, or a single eye." He provides his evidence of this Supernova, which has the appearance of the third eye between two larger eyes – like the human body — as a "fulfillment of ancient prophetic writings." [9]

Have you ever heard the story in the Book of Daniel of Daniel in the Lions Den, and Shadrach, Meshach and Abednigo in the furnace?

Daniel was delivered by the Lion.

Shadrach, Meshach and Abednigo were joined by the fourth person (God/Spirit) through the fire of the furnace. In your body the Pineal Gland is Leo the Lion, and the Fornix of the brain is the vault or furnace.

In the Universe the Pineal Gland is now displayed by Supernova 1987a, which is presently on fire.

If you will look at a picture of it you will clearly see the center single eye, which is on fire.

The Fornix of the brain is represented by the constellation 'Fornax' which is the furnace.
In the body the energy or fire from the Pineal travels along the Stria Pinealis, straight line of the Pineal, to the Fornix where it ignites the fire of the furnace bringing to us the fourth person or Christ/Spirit consciousness.

You may confirm the connection of the Pineal and Fornix via stria pinealis in Stedman's Dictionary.

In the Universe Supernova 1987a is on fire.

The fire from Supernova 1987a will travel as a fuse to Fornax the furnace, and bring to the Universe the new mind, the new consciousness, and the Christ consciousness.

In the story the fourth man appeared in the furnace when it was heated 7 times hotter which represents the 7 chakras or 7 seals.
What is a confirming fact is that on 6-10-98 there was an article from the Associated Press that astronomers had for the first time cracked the curtain of interstellar dust known as the Zone of Avoidance that blocked Earth's view of a FOURTH of the Universe.
The ancient myth is being acted out in the sky.
As well as in the human brain.
The coming fire has been misinterpreted by many as an Armageddon to destroy the Earth.
Not so.

The fire is actually the light to destroy that which is destroying the Earth.
To burn away the dross (impurity) so as to reveal the gold.[10]

Jacob's Wrestling Match

———————— • ————————

I'VE GOT ONE MORE CONCEPT to share with you concerning the spiritual aspects of the Pineal Gland. This is also from the website, Hiddenmeanings.com [11]

> *Did you ever see the old Biblical story of Jacob*
> *wrestling with the man?*
> *The man puts Jacob's thigh out and when he does,*
> *Jacob's name is changed from Jacob to Israel.*
>
> *Breaking the code reveals a pretty neat truth.*
> *Jacob wrestling with a man is you and I wrestling*
> *with ourselves.*
> *You know the inner struggles we have.*
>
> *When Jacob's thigh is put out it means desire to*
> *control the issue is gone.*

The thigh is a symbol of desire (for obvious reasons).
Now we submit to divine mind.
As soon as Jacob is no longer in control, divine mind
rules. His name is changed from Jacob to Israel.

What is Israel?
No, it's not a country.
IS = Isis. The feminine principle - Spirit
RA = Ra. The light, masculine- Mind
EL = God The supreme universal light

Thus by allowing his own desires to be broken,
Jacob is now Israel
Is— Spirit and Ra— Mind come together and
produce El— God within.

And you know the great part of this?
In Genesis 32:30 Jacob says,
"I have seen God face to face and I shall call this
place Peniel".

The pineal gland of the brain. The third eye.

The receptor of light. The fire of meditation.

The true pathway to IS RA EL.

Kundalini

———————•———————

ANOTHER PART OF THE AMAZING PROCESS of ascension is Kundalini and Kundalini energy. I can tell you for fact when most people, especially Christians, hear or see words like this it spooks them. This is probably because it is mainly spoken about and taught in the Eastern religions. In fact, the word Kundalini is Sanskrit meaning coiled, like a snake or serpent, and its beginning was in ancient Indian philosophy.

In my own words Kundalini is being able to open up your chakras, which I've just explained are your seven portals, or energy centers, running up from the base of your spine where the energy is based to the tip of your head. Once these are opened you can harness the energy that is around you at all times. It's there; you can feel it, you just can't see it. Have you ever had goose bumps and the hair on your body stands up? This is from the energy around you and inside of you. When it reaches your head, after moving through the chakras, it is said that this energy will impact the pineal gland and bring forth a spiritual enlightenment.[12]

The energy can be activated through Kundalini meditation or through the specific type of yoga called Kundalini Yoga. Some people also believe that extreme emotional situations, like a near-death experience, can stimulate the energy. And it is also believed by some followers that Kundalini energy can activate spontaneously.

Kundalini energy is also said to be very strong and can produce effects that can be overwhelming, with accompanying bright lights, strange physical sensations, visions and even pain.

The result of tapping into your Kundalini energy can include activation of your DNA, an important part of ascension. Other results include increasing clairvoyant or clairaudient capabilities; feeling connected to the oneness of the universe; feeling an expansion of the mind in your quest for higher awareness and knowledge and experiencing feelings of unconditional love, peace and connection with spirit. [13]

When it comes to learning about our bodies and practicing self-healing, Western philosophy for the most part says go to the doctor and get a prescription. We don't have time to take care of ourselves.

I have never taken yoga or anything like it. I used to practice Kung Fu and a few other martial arts with our strength and flexibility coach during my playing days in Philadelphia. There have been many times when I would push my physical body to complete exhaustion and still be able to tap into the mind and find more energy.

The figure that we see in medical pictures with the snake wrapped around the rod – the caduceus - was originated way before modern medicine. This ancient figure represents the energy coiled around your chakras, which run up your spine. When functioning properly this energy is the healing process for all four of your bodies as I described: the physical, spiritual, emotional and etheric.

I found an interesting story about Kundalini and the serpent at the website www.hiddenmeanings.com.[14] It's an interesting thought.

"The Serpent

How wonderful it is when we peek beyond the literal meaning in ancient scripture and look for the dark sayings or hidden meanings.

There is a wonderful encounter in the Bible between God and Moses.

Exodus 4:3, Moses is not sure of himself, he doesn't know what to do or what to say.
God says to Moses. Throw down your rod.
When he does the rod becomes a serpent.

Of course this is a myth with a deep meaning. Obviously a rod cannot become a serpent.
Oh yes it can.
Now look beyond the words.

The rod is the spine.
It is the symbol of the self.
IT holds us up and directs our path.

Here we are told to throw down the rod. In other words do not depend on the self.
Seek a higher consciousness above the self.
Enter into meditation. And what happens when we do.
When we enter into meditation and attain cosmic consciousness, we are no longer dependent on the rod or self, and the rod or (spine) becomes the coiled serpent, Kundalini.
At that point we who have been confused and unsure, become enlightened and are able to lead others to the glorious promised land of the new millennium mind.

So throw down your rod and guaranteed, it will become a serpent."

You are connected fully to both your Mother Earth and Father Heaven. This energy comes out of the Earth, coils up your spine and out through the top of your head. As you become more familiar with this and are able to raise your level of vibration you can feel this sensation.

I'm sure you have felt the tingling at the top of your head at some time or other. How about static electricity? How are we able to rub our feet on the carpet and then touch someone and actually see a spark? How about pulling clothes out of a dryer and having them stick to your body? Trust me folks, the energy is all around us and it's not difficult to understand once you are aware of the simple facts. At one time people thought the world was flat. Then they learned the facts. This is not voodoo; this is your divine right heritage of being able to harness all of the gifts that are presented to us. The forces of darkness have kept this information from us because they know that once we awaken to it they no longer can control us.

The Mer-Ka-Ba
(The Human Light Body)

———————— • ————————

ONCE WE ARE ABLE TO OPEN UP OUR CHAKRAS and allow energy into and through us, which enables kundalini, we are able to form our human light bodies called Mer-Ka-Ba.

Mer-Ka-Ba is said to be another of the vehicles of ascension upon the activation of its energy in and around the body. Its concept dates from Ancient Egypt and in that language the term Mer-Ka-Ba is actually three words: "Mer" is a special kind of light, a counter rotating field of light; "Ka" means spirit (at least here on Earth it has the connotation of the human spirit); and "Ba" means "the interpretation of reality" or which here on Earth usually means the human body. (Therefore it is also referred to as "body.")

When you add these words together, the understanding of Mer-Ka-Ba is "a counter rotating field of light that would take the spirit and the body from one world into another."[15] This description is from the writings of physicist and researcher Drunvalo Melchizedek, who is considered by some to have brought Mer-Ka-Ba to current consciousness with his book, "The Ancient Secret of the Flower of Life." [16]

This energy is stimulated through the breathing and visualization in Mer-Ka-Ba meditation. During this meditation process, some people are able to activate the light body and produce the energy field that begins to rotate thereby enabling them to travel to higher dimensions.

Physically the shape of Mer-Ka-Ba is described by Melchizedek as a Star Tetrahedron, like two intertwined, three-dimensional Star of David. It is my understanding that the Mer-Ka-Ba energy field, which is non-visible to the eye, extends far beyond each side of the human body, in what I believe is the form that some people correlate to what an alien disc-shaped spaceship might look like. There must be something to this particular shape that is conducive to this energy field.

Once you learn about energy, electromagnetism and all of the other components that make up our universe, you will no doubt have a better understanding of how everything works and how everything is connected. This knowledge, that most of us have never been taught, will allow you to realize that these so called myths and mysteries are nothing more than fundamental facts that are very much a part of creation. Universal energy is free and has been here since creation. The only way it will be implemented into our society is by a change in mass consciousness.

Again, everything that we require to live on this planet Earth is free. We got duped into turning this into a commercialized market.

DNA and Awakening

——————— • ———————

MOST PEOPLE HAVEN'T A CLUE ABOUT what DNA really is or what purpose it has in our bodies, other than what they have been taught in basic school science classes or heard on a TV crime show. I didn't. All I knew about DNA was that it is a basic part of our genes and is what our physical bodies are made of. This is the biological part of DNA. I was not aware of the spiritual part of DNA, but when I started researching I found out how it was and why it's so important.

To understand the part that DNA plays in ascension, it's good to start with understanding more about it. Basically, DNA is short for deoxyribonucleic acid, the nucleic acid that is the genetic material determining the makeup of all living cells and many viruses. It consists of two long strands of nucleotides linked together in a structure resembling a ladder twisted into a spiral.[17]

Most of us have seen photos of DNA, with these two long spiraling strands connected by crossing strands. This is what is known as the double helix. The two strands are the physical – or biological - property of DNA.

But here's why you need to know more about it. Many people believe that there are, in fact, at least 10 more strands of DNA that are sometimes called "Shadow DNA." Some people think there are more, even as high as 1,024 strands. Science has been perplexed for years as to what this so called Shadow—or Junk—DNA is. It is these 10 strands or more that are the spiritual, or other dimensional aspects of DNA that when activated allow us to ascend and experience other dimensions.

I believe that our DNA is changing and we are transforming from 2-strand to the higher 10 (or more) strand DNA. I also concur with what I've found in my research that, along with this, the human entity is transforming from a 2-strand carbon-based form to a crystalline based entity. It is only a crystalline based form that can ascend to a higher dimension than 3D and as our DNA transforms we can become awakened to these higher realms.[18] In the higher realms everything is of a crystalline form. Everything is absolutely beautiful and, from what I could perceive, transparent. You can visualize structure but you can also move right through it.

This transformation is taking place in the universe and with you. Whether you know it or not your DNA is changing so you can eventually be able to traverse like Jesus did. Jesus obviously gives us the best interpretation of being able to traverse into both the physical and non-physical worlds. He describes the condition of his different bodies and reveals that he can be in his physical body, yet ascend into heaven virtually at will.

There is so much energy bombarding us right now that it is changing all of us, but we aren't aware of it. Well, the majority isn't. I know the physical and mental changes that I have personally gone through and continue to go through that are my own evidence of this transformation.

I can literally be knocked on my butt for a week, kids home from school, ears hurting, flu-like symptoms, can't get out of bed, and the like. Pick up the phone and someone all the way across the country is experiencing the same thing. This kind of thing has been happening for your whole life and it continues to be very prevalent now. I'm here to tell you folks, it isn't a virus that traveled 3000 miles in a matter of minutes; it's the energy that is changing all of us. You don't get colds and flu because the temperature changes, there is a change in the energy that is affecting your bodies. I'm not saying a virus can't do that, I'm just explaining another way what can and is happening.

How is our DNA activated so that awakening can happen? One way is by the Kundalini energy that I wrote about previously. Another way is through numeric codes that trigger the genetic memory in DNA and open the "digital door."[19]

Within our physical bodies our consciousness is affected by the numbers – the numeric patterns or specific numbers – we encounter. Our DNA can be activated with repetitive numbers such as a countdown from 10 to 0 or the pattern of the Fibonacci Theorem, or through the master numbers of 11 or 22. Numbers with two digits are believed to have a greater power in our awakening than those with only one digit.

These digital codes spark our mind to awaken and return to a higher and expanded consciousness and level of awareness. The activation of our DNA by the digital codes helps us to find "clarity, healing and balance."[20] Our sense of time and the message to move on in our ascension process, comes with this. We may now feel and understand more about our mission.

After experiencing this new and, possibly sudden, awakening with the triggering of your digital codes, your reality will never be the same. As I have told you, it is very likely to be a journey that you will take alone, as your friends and colleagues may not be able to get what is happening to you. Unless, that is, it is something they are also experiencing.

At this point in history all is being revealed. Something about this Holy Spirit being poured on us is a pretty cool time to be living. I haven't been led to find the correct answer as of yet. Previously what I would do when something came up would be to dwell on it. Now, I don't consciously dwell on it, it just never goes away. This normally means that I am to ultimately receive a final answer as to what I'm supposed to learn.

DNA is consciousness, it is ascension, it is you, and it is what changes to allow transformation in all of us. Think about it. When our DNA goes back to 12 strands or more we will be able to transport just like they did on Star Trek!

11:11

———————— • ————————

IMAGINE THIS: You wake up while sleeping and glance at the clock and it reads 11:11. You get up the next morning and go through the house looking for dirty laundry lying around only to notice that one of the wall clocks in another room needs new batteries, it has stopped on 11:11. You go outside to pick up the morning paper and the sports page cover shows a game that was tied up 11 to 11 in the 11th inning before someone hit the game winner. Most likely they will have a picture of the hero and yes you guessed it, his number is 11.

Now, just as this recurring number has your attention you glance up and are looking right at the house across the street and the numbers on the garage are 1111. Now you are actually consciously going to look for it again and low and behold the car driving by has 1111 on its license plate.

This is a simple scenario to inform you of what an 11:11

experience is like: Very bizarre folks, but I already told you that truth is stranger than fiction! The 11:11 awakening is something that I experienced in the past and still do. There are other numbers that I see on a daily basis that are also part of the reprogramming of my DNA. Again, everyone is different and might have different Master Numbers specifically for them.

But what is it about the number 11 that makes it significant, not only for me but for many other people? It has been written that eleven is a higher octave of the number two, that it carries psychic vibrations and that is has an equal balance of masculine and feminine properties." [21]   It is said to contain the gift of psychic awareness, intuition, honesty and sensitivity as well, and holds the key – or trigger - to unlock our subconscious mind and let us know that we are experiencing the ascension process.

I have briefly discussed the 11:11 awakening to the public but as usual some people who think they know it all allow their egos to stick their proverbial foot in their mouths. Hopefully, though, you can begin to understand the importance of the number 11 as it relates to my experience and from what I've given you here, to help you realize that there may be this or another number significant to you.

Trust me this is a no-brainer. If it happens you will know because you can't avoid it. It's divinely appointed for you when your soul is ready. As stated earlier, your life will take on a whole new meaning and you will realize even though we have free will down here, our creator is still in control of His/Her precious cargo.

I would like to share one more thing about the number 11 and the power of its awakening mankind to his divinity. The 9/11 tragedy was one of those events that happened to help awaken mankind. Of course there are conspiracy theories surrounding it but I'm not here to discuss that. Conspiracies have always been here and always will until everyone's level of consciousness is raised so they no longer exist in society. I have had my day in the sun with the powers that be about conspiracies and no longer care to engage in rhetoric that doesn't concern me. I have a job to do and will leave the conspiracy stuff to the ones who are inclined to pursue.

However, I do believe that there is a mathematical equation to everything created or else there would be randomness and coincidences. There is an exactness of perfection in what our creator created; not one flaw. Every major incident in our lives was allowed into motion for our experience in this density, no matter how wonderful or horrible it was perceived. They happen so we can learn but if we continue to recreate the same mistakes we will forever be stuck in the 3rd dimension.

Soon after the 9/11 tragedy, this information that follows about the number 11 and the way it related to that day surfaced and was widely sent around the internet. Some people dismiss this as coincidence or contrivance but I, like may others, see the symbolism differently.

THE NUMBER 11 AND THE 9/11 TRAGEDY

The date of the attack: 9/11: 9+1+1=11.

Mohammed's birth is celebrated on the 11th day of the 9th month.

September 11th is the 254th day of the year: 2+5+4=11.

After September 11th there are 111 days left to the end of the year.

119 is the area code to Iraq/Iran. 1+1+9=11.

Twin Towers standing side by side look like the number 11.

The number of stories is 110 (2x) 110 – 110

Remember that "0" is not a number, so we have 11:11.

The number of Tower windows = 21,800 - 2+1+8= 11.

The third building #7 to fall had 47 stories = 4+7=11.

The first plane to hit the towers was flight 11.

American Airlines number 1-800-245-0999

1+8+0+0+2+4+5+0+9+9+9 = 47 = 11

State of New York – The 11th State added to the Union

New York City – 11 letters

Afghanistan – 11 letters

The Pentagon – 11 letters

Ramzi Yousef – 11 letters (convicted of orchestrating the bombing attack on the WTC in 1993)

George W. Bush – 11 letters

Flight 11 – 92 on board – 9+2+11

Flight 11 had 11 crewmembers.

Flight 77 – 65 on board – 6+5 = 11.

The Flight 11 call letters were AA11: A=1, A=1, AA=11.

Four of the hijackers on Flight AA11 have the initials A.A. for their names: AA=11.

The fifth hijacker was the pilot, Mohamed Atta, 11 letters, and AA in last name.

Flight AA11 had 92 people on board – 9+2=11

Manhattan Island was discovered on Sept. 11, 1609 by Henry Hudson – 11 letters.

Trade Center is 11 letters and Skyscrapers is 11 letters.

The first WTC tower hit (North Tower) collapses at 10:28 A.M. –   1+2+8=11.

The 1st Fire Unit to arrive at the WTC towers was FDNY Unit1. Unit 1 lost 11 Firemen.

The WTC towers collapsed to a height of 11 stories.

On Sept. 7, 2002, NYC Medical Examiners announced the revised official death toll from the WTC attacks was 2,801 – (2+8+0+1=11). [22]

I will voice my opinion from a multi-dimensional being living in a multi-dimensional world that the souls that were taken in the 9/11 tragedy were a part of the reincarnation process (more on this topic later) and were to be a part of that event prior to reincarnating. In no way do I mean to lessen the seriousness of the tragedy or to diminish the devastation of the loss of lives, or offend the grieving friends and families of the souls taken. These souls didn't die; they passed on to higher realms, a higher way of being. This has to be, this is Universal Law in the 3rd density. We live in duality, polarity, black and white, good and evil, positive and negative.

This event, however, may have shocked and awakened people to the extent of their taking off the blinders, that Big Brother isn't the security blanket that we've always expected. It taught us to look elsewhere for that security, which in my opinion is either up or within. Most of us look up but hopefully by the end of this book you will realize that whatever you're looking up for is actually within.

This event was so huge that it had a major impact on the world and our awakening. We as humans have a propensity to forget things and end up doing them again and again. I don't think we will be forgetting this tragedy anytime soon.

You will no doubt find a lot of information about the demonic side of this tragic event. It's there, always has been and always will be in this dimension. Again, this dimension is of duality and polarities. You would never know there was light if you have never experienced darkness and vice versa.

I have experienced what we would term as demonic encounters just like in the movie *The Exorcist*. [23] Why? I believe it was for my spiritual growth and more importantly I was ready for it when it happened. It can be a very frightening experience. You will also realize these energies and the spiritual laws that must be adhered to concerning what we perceive to be demonic possession.

I don't mean to belittle the situation by describing it as something we perceive, but it really is something of our perception. Don't get me wrong; it is very real at the moment of the experience.

Remember, everything created is light; some things are denser than others. These darker, denser forces are unable to travel beyond the 4th density. I could be wrong on this but my personal experience leads me to believe that until you lose your density, which in essence is your negative characteristics, you are unable to go beyond the 4th dimension.

This only makes sense as manifesting your every thought occurs in the 4th dimension. This is very spooky and therefore we aren't allowed to ascend higher until our negativity is released or we would be re-creating all of the miserable things we have already experienced. I will tell more and give examples later.

Back to the number 11. The 11:11 awakening is very real and I'm not sure how many people this particular number has an effect on. I have read much on it and have met people who have also experienced it, but for the most part it doesn't seem to have hit the masses. I believe we are all wired differently, therefore different strokes for different folks. I also believe that everyone has a particular number, symbol, sign or something similar that triggers their own personal awakening.

Now you have a pretty good idea what the 11:11 awakening is all about. I hope you get my point and I also hope it will happen to you soon because it is really neat. There are way more examples than what is here and much more information about this on the internet and in bookstores. If you care to indulge and learn more there is plenty of information concerning disasters and numbers, dates, times and location on the global grids. Almost seems like a MATRIX we live in!

4.

"And it shall come to pass afterward, that I will pour out my spirit upon all flesh; and your sons and your daughters shall prophesy, your old men shall dream dreams, your young men shall see visions..."

Joel 2:28

Dimensions and Reality

———————— • ————————

WHAT IS REALITY? MOST PEOPLE FEEL THAT being born, growing up, going to school, having a career, growing old and dying is reality. Most, also feel that depending on how you lived your life and how you treated people you will either go to Heaven or Hell when you die. Wrong! When we were created it was forever. Eternal doesn't die. We have been duped into believing that this life we consciously know of is all there is. This is why there is so much fear surrounding death. We don't die folks; we just pass on to another realm. Granted, your physical body returns to dust but your soul, who is actually who you are, continues to evolve.

How do I know? Because I've consciously been in these other realms—astral travel while in a sleeping state and conscious experiences during the day, while awake. At first it was very strange because I wasn't privy to how or why this new world opened up to me. I wanted to tell people but I wasn't well versed in how it all worked.

When I first went public with my experiences of traveling in other dimensions, people looked at me, and talked about me, as if I came from outer space. I guess the most difficult part of it all for me has been figuring out a way to explain to them what they are and what each are capable of because some people are in serious denial. You just have to connect the dots of what myself and others are trying to convey to you concerning entering these realms. First of all you have to believe it and that you're capable of doing it. If you don't get past the first step I can assure you it's not going to happen.

After a few years of my being awakened and experiencing these higher realms on a daily basis, things are really awesome. I still can't talk to some people about it without their ego ruining what could be an awesome learning experience but there are many more people who are listening.

Why are people so afraid of something they know nothing about? I can honestly say that I have never lost any sleep or been offended over some news about extraterrestrial beings or something beyond our five senses. I've been envious yes, but never offended or feeling inferior.

At the present moment the life that each of us lives is a level of consciousness in a certain one of the dimensions or plane of existence I've described. There are many of these dimensions around us at all times and – here's the real shocker - you live in all of these different dimensions at the same time. You are just not consciously aware of this. You cannot consciously see these dimensions because you aren't vibrating on the same frequency. Until you are able to raise your level of consciousness the only reality that you are aware of is this one in 3D.

This gets really good so hang with me! When our Father/Mother Creator created, He/She wanted us to experience all of what was created; therefore this is where we come in. We are all soul sparks from our creator. (I use both the Masculine and Feminine when I reference our Creator because we are both.) I realize that we all feel the separation from our creator as well as everyone and everything else but this is the illusion that can only be comprehended by experiencing the higher realms.

Jesus tried to teach this to the masses back then and they couldn't comprehend it. Even his Disciples couldn't understand what he was telling them. Honestly, you aren't supposed to until your soul is mature enough to handle it. Remember when he said you will be fed milk as a child until you are able to digest the meat.

Just as we split as soul sparks from our creator and came down to the lower realms for this experience, our souls split as well into all of these other dimensions. Just like our creator, we fragmented into many different soul sparks so we could experience living in all of the realms, just like our creator is experiencing through all of us. What is above is as below. Remember Jesus saying, "I AM" when they asked who he was? There is no separation in "I AM." You are living in all of the realms too, you just don't know it. It's kind of neat though knowing that we get to experience just like he does. The only difference is we are at the moment unaware of the other realms we live in.

When we fall asleep, however, we get to experience all of these other realms. We cannot yet comprehend what dreaming is. When we wake and remember our dreams we wonder, what the heck was that all about? Folks, know this as truth. Our dreams are reality in other realms. Our dream state is actually the best reality because we aren't restricted to the flesh. We travel at our every whim, no rush hour traffic, no lines, no taxes, no bull#&%*!! Problem is when we come back into our body; we pierce the proverbial veil again and are restricted from all the juicy stuff. Not for long, folks. Trust me on this one, the veil is thinning and we aren't far off from gaining ALL of it.

There are many references in the Bible concerning ascension and entering these other realms of existence. Most notable was Jesus' Ascension to and from, and the different bodies we have that when mature enough can travel back and forth in these realms.

Paul was taken up but wasn't sure if he was in his body or not.

Probably the most difficult thing to comprehend is that everything we perceive is in our minds and we are unable to understand the veil of illusion associated with reality. What if I told you that the realms you are unable to see - the spiritual realms - are actually where we come from? This lower realm, the 3rd density is actually an illusion. I know, you think I'm crazy but I assure you I'm not. For me it is very difficult to describe this, as the mind of God is way beyond our means. There are others that have much more knowledge and wisdom that can explain it better but I will give it a shot.

Everything in creation is a form of energy. God is pure energy, not just a man in the form of Jesus or an older looking man with gray hair and a gray beard. God is the most profound light there is beyond our comprehension. He made all of the energy in the Universe that you can relate to. He/She is everything and therefore everything has the building blocks of creation in it, even the things you cannot see such as protons, neutrons and electrons.

When he created, God said "Let there be light."(Gen. 1:3, RSV) We know that sound is very prevalent in creation and sound is vibration. Everything is a form of energy, which is actually a certain level of light or density. The brightest light and most intense energy comes from our Creator, The Source. The closer you are to source, the more light and energy you obtain. The farther away you get from source the less light and energy, hence more density.

When you feel close to God, you know when you just experienced something magical in your life. You feel wonderful and full of energy. This is because you have opened yourself up to him and he is filling you up with the Holy Spirit, or pure divine energy. On the contrary, when you are miserable and going through negativity in your life, you have actually closed off these chakras I spoke about earlier and are unable to receive that precious life force. Your mind controls your destiny: Think positive, receive positive. Think negative, receive negative.

O.K., we're getting there. As dimensions and levels of vibration go, we are in the 3rd density or dimension. Everything in the 3rd dimension that you can touch is made of matter, which means that whatever it is that you are touching is vibrating at a slower rate than light. We can see light but cannot feel it unless of course it is generating heat. You can slip your hand through a flashlight beam but you cannot run your hand through the television. This means that light is vibrating at a faster rate than your solid TV.

Let's go a step further. When you are listening to your radio, how are you able to turn the dial and go from hearing a station in Los Angeles to one in New York? Energy is everywhere; in televisions, radios, microwaves, gamma, beta and theta rays; all kinds. You get my point. We are literally inundated with different kinds of energy waves. These waves are how information and communication travel instantaneously. Do I need to say anymore than the World Wide Web?

The difference in listening to one station and being able to get to another one is the level at which they are vibrating. It is the same principle when you are going from the 3rd dimension to the fourth, fifth, sixth, or higher. Remember, your reality is all in your mind, therefore to raise your level of consciousness and tap into another reality you have to accomplish all of the criteria I mentioned before. This isn't some spooky sci-fi movie, this is real and we all can and will do it.

Your soul spark or receiver of energy is already in these other dimensions at all times. All that is required is for you to send out the signal on the correct frequency and voila, you tap into another one of those "Mansions" that Jesus was talking about. Trust me it's not easy to do, as you have to lose all of the negative energy that you've been carrying around for eons. It is my understanding that one has to continue to lose the darkness (density) to continue to climb back up the proverbial ladder, rung by rung. In other words you cannot jump from the 3rd density to the 12th overnight.

I know you're thinking how is this possible? Well, don't ask me

I am just the messenger. I can tell you again, everything around us has the building blocks of creation in it, even the tiny little things that you can't see.

Have you ever seen a Hologram? All of creation is holographic, meaning that if you took a tiny part of the whole Universe it would indeed contain the same amount of information and energy as the whole. In essence it doesn't matter where you are; you still are everywhere and in everything.

It's easier to try and comprehend this from a quantum view, which is again, the things you can't see, but are no less there. How does information travel instantaneously from one part of the globe to another part 6,000 miles away? How do the people who are telepathic have the ability to instantly communicate with their minds with someone across the globe? We are connected and trust me, we can obtain some amazing powers! Just start believing.

Our Heavenly Father said he was omnipotent, omnipresent, and omniscient; everything, everywhere, all-knowing. SO ARE WE!

What You Can Expect in the Higher Realms

———————•———————

BEFORE I EXPLAIN SOME OF MY PERSONAL experiences in the other realms, I want to make sure we are on the same page as to how this is possible. Remember, reality as we experience it comes from our minds, which in essence is the mind of God. Our current reality is energy that is manifested in the 3rd dimension. We are co-creators and have the ability to create our own reality. We collectively have created the reality that we all live in, in this density. If we collectively changed our ways of thinking we could instantaneously change our reality.

I would like to share a story about collective consciousness and how it works on the grids surrounding everything. It is a story about what is called the "100th Monkey Theory" that originally comes from a book *Lifetide* by Dr. Lyall Watson.[24] The version below is from the book *The Hundredth Monkey* by Ken Keyes, Jr.[25] Some people consider the story to be folklore and others that the story, or some version of a spontaneous leap of consciousness, occurred.

The Japanese monkey, Macaca Fuscata had been observed in the wild for a period of over thirty years. These particular scientists were feeding this monkey sweet potatoes.

The monkey liked the potatoes but found the dirt unpleasant. An 18 month old female named Imo found she could solve the problem by washing the potatoes in a nearby stream. She taught this trick to her mother. Her playmates also learned this new way and they taught their mothers too.

This cultural innovation was gradually picked up by various monkeys before the eyes of the scientists. Between 1952 and 1958 all the young monkeys learned to wash the sandy sweet potatoes to make them more palatable. Only the adults who imitated their children learned this social improvement. Other adults kept eating their dirty sweet potatoes.

Then something startling took place. In the autumn of 1958, a certain number of Koshima monkeys were washing their potatoes. The exact number was not known. Let us suppose that when the sun arose one morning there were 99 monkeys who had learned to wash their potatoes. Let's further suppose that later that morning, the 100th monkey also learned to wash potatoes.

Then It Happened!

By the evening almost everyone in the tribe was washing their potatoes before eating them. The added energy of the 100th monkey somehow created an ideological breakthrough.

But notice: A most surprising thing observed by the scientist was that the habit of washing these potatoes jumped over the sea. Colonies of monkeys on other islands and the mainland troop of monkeys at Takisakiyama began washing their potatoes. Thus, when a certain critical number achieves awareness, this new awareness can be communicated from mind to mind.

Although the exact number may vary, this 100th monkey phenomenon means that when only a limited number of people know of a new way, it may remain a conscious property of these people. But there is a point at which, if only one more person tunes in to a new awareness, a field is strengthened so that this awareness is picked up by almost everyone.

It will take an enormous amount of energy to change conscious reality that we have created though. I have read where it takes at least 144,000 souls to collectively manifest significant change. I don't know this for sure and I have other opinions of the spiritual metaphor concerning the 144,000 written of in the Bible. (Rev. 7:3-8; Rev. 14:3, RSV)

However, that's the way energy works and our every thought is very powerful energy. Whenever you get in a rut the first thing you should think about is what exactly am I thinking about that is allowing me to remain in this rut. Change your mind and focus your energy on something positive and you will get out of that rut.

When you start your ascension into the higher realms, your number one action is changing your ways and getting outside of society's box. Think of the big picture that I have told you about, not the daily grind, paying bills and the like. Dwelling on these is a barrier. Another stumbling block could be your desire of wanting fame and fortune in this world. There's nothing wrong with that, I'm just saying it will keep you tied to the 3rd dimension. The thoughts of this dimension are lower vibrating thoughts. I am suggesting desiring all if it. Remember, money and material things are of this physical dimension, which are nice to have, but have the desire for all of your divinity. I know this is easier said than done because the 3rd dimension and the powers that are allowed to control have duped us into the all mighty dollar. I certainly have felt victimized by this but trust me it is all an illusion. It's not real and we can consciously rise above it.

If you want to see things with your eyes closed, experience astral travel or traveling through time, be clairaudient, clairvoyant, or acquire telepathy — basically all the things you did before you chose to come down — start by reprogramming yourself. You've done all of these things a million times. It's like riding a bike. Start thinking about these gifts you already have and watch the 100th monkey theory kick in. All of us will be "flying" around the place. It's damn better than sitting in traffic, I can tell you that! I'm drop-dead serious about this. I know some of this stuff better than baseball, and I know baseball. Just stop limiting yourself. The whole problem is people saying you can't do it. You can do it. It's possible but you must believe.

Metaphysics:
Planes of Existence
and Piercing the Veil

———————— • ————————

THAT WHICH VIBRATES SLOWER THAN the speed of light is what we call the material plane. That which vibrates faster than the speed of light we call the metaphysical plane.

Those vibrations just faster than the speed of light are the astral planes. The astral plane is the plane of emotions. Move the vibrations up higher and you get the mental planes. The lower to middle mental planes are where our conscious minds function. Raise the level of vibration higher and you are in the spiritual realm. Raise the level higher and you connect directly with source.

One of the most difficult times in my life was when I first started piercing the veil and moving through these planes. My old life was in shambles and I started experiencing what I will say is the 4th dimension. Now remember, all that requires one to tap into another reality is a change in your frequency or vibration just like turning the dial on your radio.

As I have mentioned before, at this time there were things that happened in my life that I—or anyone—couldn't have possibly planned on doing and have them all actually come true. If your life is completely upside down and you have absolutely no idea how these kinds of things could possibly be happening to you, you might be close to piercing the veil. It might be your time. Ask anyone who has seen the other realms and I'll bet that their story is similar.

A problem you might run into, such as happened to yours truly, is you can be experiencing both the 3rd and 4th realms at the same time consciously. Experiencing both of these dimensions at the same time is very confusing and can be very uncomfortable. You could be having a conversation with someone at dinner physically in the 3rd dimension, but your mind is vibrating consciously in the 4th. The person next to you could ask you a question but your mind is engaged in some activity in another plane of existence.

Let me explain this because I already told you that another you is already in this other realm, you just needed a frequency change to hook up with this other you. It's like when you change your dial and it is resting right in between two different radio stations. You can hear what's going on in both channels, correct, except it's definitely distorted.

Now, apply that same scenario to two different planes of existence. Trust me; there are others who have experienced this. I have read enough books to know that others went through the same thing and some of the people did take their lives. This will be the most bizarre experience you have ever consciously encountered if you get stuck between both.

This actually lasted for a while with me mainly because everything in my life was so negative at the time. The only real pleasure I had was when I was with my children, which wasn't often enough. I had trouble dumping enough "luggage" to raise my consciousness a little higher to remain in the higher plane so I got to experience both at the same time for a while.

What's it like you ask? Figured I'd have to relive the old negative experiences. Don't forget I was still in the 3rd dimension where everything looks, smells, tastes, feels and sounds the same as always. I woke up everyday and lived like always although at the time I was pretty miserable.

If this happens to you, and I mean this, first of all you better hide all of the sharp objects. Because you are a brand spanking new player in a game you know nothing about, you may want to take the easy way out. This is one of the reasons I felt impelled to tell people about this.

Let me describe the 4th dimension to you. The weird part about the 4th dimension is it is kind of the spiritual battleground. Vibrations that are faster than the speed of light are often known as the astral plane. The 4th dimension is also the realm of emotions. It has been termed a morphogenic plane of existence. This means that you could be walking along and look at a tree and it could actually change into appearing to be an animal right before your very eyes. For that matter it can change into whatever your most prominent thought is in your mind. The spooky thing about this is we really haven't a clue as to what is in our subconscious mind.

If you have a lot of critters in your closet, so to speak, this is the plane where they all come out. All of the scary movies that we watch have been created from someone's mind therefore they are real in someone's subconscious world. Let me explain. When we fall asleep we pierce the veil and reenter the spiritual world. Most of the time when we awaken we cannot remember our dreams.

One thing that you must try to comprehend is whenever we sleep we travel into another plane of existence, or for that matter any dimension our soul is allowed to enter. When we wake we reenter this plane. Remember our four bodies. When you lay your physical body down to rest and regenerate, your soul steps out and continues to party on.

Remember, like attracts like, so if your life is miserable, then your soul experiences these realms we like to refer to as Hell, Hades or the bottomless pit. If life is very good then your soul is having fun in wonderful realities.

Sometimes we can remember our dreams and sometimes there is information that we bring back to assist us in our daily walk. Sometimes we awaken in the middle of a dream that scares the hell out of us. Well, where do you think your soul just left? How about having a wet dream where you wake up with the same exact feeling and result of doing "it" consciously. I implore you, which one is the real one? They all are real because you are a co-creator and you create all kinds of realities. Because of the illusion of separation in 3D we feel as if everything is already here and we are participating in it. This is untrue though; we actually create moment by moment. It's kind of like watching a movie reel. The film is made of many snapshots that pass quickly through the projector to produce the reality of the movie.

Back to the 4th dimension. My experience and further research lead me to believe that the forces of light and darkness battle in this realm. In this realm we are able to manifest at will. This is the scary part again. In the 3rd dimension everything vibrates at a slower rate, even your thoughts take awhile to manifest. In the 3rd you are born and grow up hoping to be something, and it takes awhile to achieve it. In the 4th and higher planes whatever you think automatically appears. Sound bizarre, it is bizarre and that is why we have to rid ourselves of lower density thoughts and vibrations before ascending. If not we would not only be creating the same negative experiences over again and they would be happening instantly. Why I was allowed to experience this for so long, I'm not sure other than I am supposed to write about it and tell the rest of the world. It felt like forever but I did get through it.

I'm not sure if everyone will have to experience the negative while in this realm. Like I wrote earlier I was very bitter at the time and somewhat frightened, as I couldn't figure out how everything that was going through my mind was automatically happening.

You will eventually understand how it works and how powerful your thoughts are and the fact that you are the one creating every scene in the movie.

It is like having phenomenal skills to be able to figure out just about anything that is brought to your attention but with the fact that you have no idea how it is all happening. All of the senses are enhanced dramatically and even more. You will consciously feel like you are losing your mind because quite frankly your ego has never had to deal with something like this. You can and will function in the life that you've always known, but you cannot completely go back to it.

Manifesting in the 4th Dimension
Multi-Dimensional Universe

————————— • —————————

AVE YOU EVER SEEN THE MOVIE *Multiplicity* with Michael Keaton?[26] The movie is about a normal guy that finds out there are three others that are identical to him. The concept of the movie is reality except we are unaware of ourselves in these other dimensions.

Like Michael Keaton's character, we too are multi-dimensional beings living in a multi-dimensional world. A multi-dimensional world means that the world we live in has multiple dimensions all in the same space and time, and multi-dimensional beings means we live in those dimensions — all at the same time and in the same space.

As we awaken to this reality we realize that we are everywhere at all times and can be anywhere at the instant of thought. Obviously this isn't going to happen overnight, but it is happening. Again, one reason that some people have witnessed these things and others haven't is that our souls are ready for this stuff and we are supposed to tell others. Doesn't make us any better. The Bible speaks of a veil that is around each of us. This veil cannot be something outside of us as a curtain or we would all pierce it at the same time. Each of us is different in this respect, each being on his or her time.

An experience I had opened my mind up to this reality. One day while sitting outside my beach house with a friend I noticed all of these people walking out on the beach. No big deal except that the feeling came over me again that I had slipped into another plane. The cool thing about this was I knew all of these people. I started pointing at these people, telling my friend each of their names. She asked how I knew all of these people. I told her they were friends I grew up with in Kansas. She then asked what in the heck are they doing here.

I told her that they are still in Kansas but I wondered how is it they are right here, right now. I had at this point enough of these experiences to realize that I vibrate in and out of these different realms, but how was she able to see these people? I was getting ready to walk out on the beach to say hello to these old friends and all of a sudden I saw my parents and my older brother. My jaw dropped, as this was a kick in the butt. The weird thing about this if it could possibly get any weirder was that they were 40 years younger. They looked like they did when they first got married, and my brother looked like a young kid.

No sooner did I pick my jaw up off the floor when my old baseball coach and manager Lee Elia walked by. Lee, you will probably take a lot of heat from this but I just have to tell this story because it was simply awesome. I have no idea why you were part of this experience. All I know is it was completely real. I also wish I could tell you that you looked 40 years younger but I can't, you looked the same as now and you were kind of gimping around on that bad knee. Nice tan though and damn you are hairy!

As amazing as all of this seems, it gets better. I looked out towards the water and couldn't take my eyes off of this guy running on the beach…it was ME! Identical. I watched as I ran down the beach out of sight. I sat there in amazement as to why I was experiencing this one. I wanted to go out on the beach and touch these people to see if they were real but something came over me to just sit there and take this in because it would be ending in a minute. Then, everyone just kind of picked up their things and slowly walked off the beach as if they had been there all day.

I felt as if this whole performance was specifically played out just for my ability to learn about our being multi-dimensional beings living in multiple dimensions. People, one thing you must do is train your mind to believe that we have these multiple dimensions around us and are in them all. What exactly does that mean, you ask? I'm not sure if I can explain it that well. I only know it because I've seen it and experienced it. Needless to say I hit the books and the internet to learn more about this phenomenon.

It's kind of like the hologram I was talking about earlier. A hologram is comprised of many little pieces that are all the same, yet when they are connected they form the whole. Even if you remove any piece, it will still contain the whole of what you are visualizing. All of creation is a hologram. If you take one little micron that you cannot see with the naked eye it still contains all of creation in it. I realize it might be very difficult for your mind to understand this but it might be easier once you realize that matter is really an illusion and that everything is light, just different degrees of light.

Here's a perfect example to illustrate what we are and what is happening. Have you ever had Déjà vu? Déjà vu is experiencing the overlapping of more than one dimension. Let me repeat myself; Déjà vu is experiencing the overlapping of more than one dimension.

A Déjà vu experience is not a coincidence. There is no such thing as a coincidence in this creation; know this for a fact as there never has been and never will be. That would mean that there is randomness and chaos. Our creator is unable to create that. Every thought has a definitive mathematical equation to its purpose.

I know most of you reading this have had Déjà vu so therefore you also have had the experience of piercing the veil into other dimensions. You are not as lame as you thought you were and if you are thinking about ripping me after reading this book, think again, because I'll rip you back because you have admitted to the same thing as I have. Sometimes it is nice to be able to laugh at yourself!

Anyway, what happens is we live lives in these other dimensions but are only conscious of living one life in this dimension. Are you with me? At this very moment you are living many different lives in many different dimensions.

Remember, in the higher realms everything is happening much quicker. There is no such thing as time in the higher planes. Everything just is. Also remember that, as we lower our vibration into the lower realms, there are sub planes in each dimension. As we lower our vibration, manifesting becomes much slower and once you reenter the plane that vibrates slower than the speed of light, we have matter. As mentioned earlier, in the 3rd dimension (the material plane), it generally takes our whole life to manifest our dreams. In the 4th density, where there are the mental planes, emotional planes and astral planes, we are able to manifest at will.

Déjà vu is experiencing something that just occurred in one of the higher planes. Living in the 3rd density, I believe we are the last of us to experience this phenomenon as the 2nd density is comprised of plants and animals, and I believe the 1st density to be comprised of the elements we know, i.e. air, earth, fire and water.

When Déjà vu occurs, it feels as if you've just experienced the same thing over again—you did. Kind of neat, huh?

Astral Travel

———————— • ————————

ASTRAL TRAVEL IS A DIMENSIONAL JOURNEY in the 4th dimension, when it is possible to leave one's physical body. You may have heard it called an "out of body" experience. The first time I experienced astral travel was in a hotel room in Naples, Florida. This experience was really incredible and was probably the most exhilarating of all the other times that I have done this. My research has led me to believe that some people are very good at this and can do it just about any time they want. Like most of the other gifts we have that I mention in this book, this is one that I have never been in control of. It just happens to me on different occasions, such as when I am lying down, just before falling asleep. I've tried to apply what I had to eat or drink, my location, whatever, in hopes to find the answer of being in control of it. We are in control of this really awesome tool but again, it's all in our minds and we must be able to raise our level of consciousness to the astral plane.

I was lying in bed not quite asleep yet but very relaxed. This wasn't a dream, folks, as I was fully conscious. At this particular time in my life I had been listening to Peter Gabriel's song "Solsbury Hill", which means "Souls Bearing Hill."[27] This is actually a physical place in England, near the City of Bath. I was pretty naïve concerning all of the things that I was experiencing. When this happened it was quite refreshing as I was searching for answers to this new world I happened to be in.

I mention that once you start the ascension process you will be led and given the answers that are needed in learning about what you are experiencing. As hairy as it gets because you are a new player in the game, you will be guided and are never alone even though you will definitely feel alone. The synchronicities of your daily walk will be very dramatic and profound and these are to inform you that you are very much connected to everything else. The problem is you probably won't be able to figure out how all of these phenomena can possibly happen and occur the way they do. It is literally magic and no one else around you will have any idea of what you are personally experiencing. This is your baby; this is your call to awaken to your divinity and all of the other magnificent realms of reality that our creator has provided us.

You will be guided with signs, symbols, sounds and connections. Everything seen and unseen will be at your whim to get you to realize the many forms of communication around you at all times. Once you experience how this works it will never leave you. It has never left me and I can assure you that this form of communication is within and around you this very moment. You are just uninformed of how it works. We presently either talk, see, listen or touch to communicate and it is primarily one at a time. When you are able to raise your consciousness just a little you will find that you can use all of them simultaneously or you will receive answers from the senses that you wouldn't normally use. Rather than hearing your answer you will be able to look at something the moment a question pops into your mind and receive the answer right in front of you. Trust me, everything is connected.

Back to the story. At this particular time I was actually baring my soul and finding out who I really am. This too will happen to you; it is inevitable. At some moment in our existence we are ultimately brought to the point of finding out whom we really are. If you listen to the words to this song, Solsbury Hill, they are very appropriate to what was being revealed to me. One part contains the words: "Pack your bags boy it's time to take you home." This was very relevant at the time because this is exactly what I felt everyday. I honestly felt that this life was over and I was going home. I just didn't know when.

As I was lying in bed I slipped into this realm consciously and I found myself on a road at night. I was in my body standing when a red car drove up to me on my left. It turned away and morphed into red wine. I then looked to my right and the red wine was being poured into a water puddle. As soon as the water turned to wine I immediately shot straight up into the air, probably a few hundred feet as I could look down and see all of the houses, trees and lights. This was so real and I shot up so fast that my stomach seemed to be in my throat. I have been on a lot of amusement rides but this one definitely took the cake.

The really weird part of this flight was that I was still standing up when all of a sudden I started soaring through the air. You must know that at this particular moment of this experience I had no idea how this was happening nor did I know where I was. I really felt that I had no control over this event until I was headed for this hill that had a bench and three crosses on top. I was traveling so fast that I thought I was going to crash into this hill so the first thing that came to me was to lie down. All of a sudden I turned over like Superman and soared right over the hill. As soon as I got back out over open land, I noticed the lights and homes below and immediately popped back into my body lying in bed in the hotel.

There was no doubt that up to that point in my life this was the coolest thing I had ever done, bar none! Way better than hitting a grand slam, this was awesome and I wanted more! As I lay there I tried to figure out how this was possible. I just took off on a trip and flew around the country at night in my body that looked just like my other body lying in bed.

The next thing that came to me was where did I just go? There was only one place I know of that has a hill with a bench and three crosses on it and it is in my hometown in Kansas. On the side of the hill the words "Christ Died for the Ungodly" are written. The size of these words is very much equivalent to the Hollywood sign in Los Angeles and can be seen for miles.

I started trying to put all of the pieces together in hopes that this would make sense. I correlated everything to that one song that I had been listening to over and over for the past few weeks. It talks about turning water into wine and finding your soul and going back home. I started getting an overwhelming feeling of being just like Jesus Christ and this stayed with me for months. I actually remember walking down a country road with my mother telling her that I feel like I am Jesus Christ. I also told her it wasn't in an egotistical way, that I wasn't actually him, just that I had the overwhelming feeling of love and devotion towards everyone and everything that he had. Please don't be misinformed as this isn't an ego trip and I certainly don't care to offend anyone.

I will however, tell you that when you start this enlightenment process you will no doubt feel this sensation. One of the ascension symptoms is described as a feeling of Christ Consciousness. This is precisely what this transformation is, having the light of Christ revealed to your conscious reality. This is what I believe the man Jesus experienced and was trying to reveal to the masses.

Once this happens you know inside that what is being revealed to you everyday is something that everyone else is not receiving. This is exactly what Jesus went through and your path from that moment forward is to share with the masses something that throughout our modern history has landed most on a cross or burned at the stake. This is the very reason Jesus said, "Forgive them Father for they know not what they do." (Luke 23:34, RSV) All of us have heard or read this statement. What exactly is it that they do not know? It is the light of Christ within each of us that must be lit to reveal true reality! Everything that we have been taught isn't even close to reality; there is way more than this earthly existence.

As I mentioned earlier this feeling of Christ Consciousness didn't enter me until I went through many months of being baptized through the fire, which I will refer to as my own "Dark Night of The Soul." This is that very lonely time where your true faith will be tested once entering the 4th density where all hell breaks loose. I have only met a few people who have experienced Christ Consciousness and our topic of conversation was how we share something that nobody believes in. I have read many books and entered many websites and all speak of the same scenario: The masses absolutely refuse to believe. There is no doubt a level of respect for this person Jesus Christ that is second to none, as there should be. This isn't the question, the question is why don't we believe in what he was teaching us and the fact that he said we could do all of the things he was doing?

We simply believe that we are human beings with five senses, we are born, grow up and die, then go to either Heaven or Hell to spend the rest of eternity. Wrong. The best one I hear all the time is when someone is lying on their death bed, somebody has to get in there and talk this guy into accepting Jesus Christ so he can go to Heaven. People, think about that for a minute; does that really make sense? Is your whole existence for the rest of eternity predicated on the sentence, "I accept Jesus Christ as my savior." If it is then what in the hell are we all fighting about? Why do we dislike convicted criminals if we can just let 'em go and make sure they say the "code words" before they die?

What about all of the other religions that don't believe in this religious context; they're out obviously. Try talking to someone who has a different faith and getting them to say the code words. Good luck. This is religion folks, no more, no less. You have chosen to separate from others because of something that has been taught to you from your family or friends for centuries. Jesus never taught that.

Jesus taught that you must become Christ-like, that is like Christ, which is the Spirit of God. Jesus was changed, transformed because of the light within him. To enter the Kingdom of Heaven which is the heavenly realm, you must first realize the light within you. The more of this Holy Spirit that you anchor within you the less darkness, or density, you obtain. The lighter you are the higher you ascend in this grand game. Once revealed you will chuckle at the way people think about life and death and what we thought was the only way. Our creator is pure spirit, pure consciousness.

BOSTON

I will share some other flights with you but I will continue to say when you have your first astral travel consciously it kind of stays with you. One night while lying in bed fully awake I took off, except this time I didn't take off like a rocket. (Again, if you do not have the complete ability to astral travel then it will most likely occur while you are in the state of not quite asleep and not quite awake.) It was dark and I just appeared to be flying over water. It seemed like everything on the banks of what looked like a river had just experienced a nuclear bomb or some other sort of devastation. I couldn't feel life anywhere. The thing that was bad was I was soaring on my back and couldn't turn over. To this day I haven't a clue why I stayed on my back, other than maybe I wasn't supposed to see much.

I recall feeling that I didn't enjoy being there so all of a sudden I took off at warp speed and flew over an ocean into a city and it was snowing. I thought and felt as if it was Boston. Why I haven't a clue other than the feeling. I flew in backwards and popped up in the middle of the street. As soon as I was standing in the street I automatically popped back into my body in bed.

As with all of these experiences, I tried to figure out the meaning or purpose of this trip and the only answer was this devastation was something in another country that is supposed to happen in the near future but I am not supposed to see it. I also thought that it could have already happened, but the thing that threw me off was when I flew into this city the buildings were tall, so it had to be in our modern era.

SACRED GEOMETRY

One particular flight happened when I had been studying Sacred Geometry during the day time. I am absolutely sure that most people have no idea what sacred geometry is or even heard of it. Sacred Geometry can be described as "*a belief system attributing a religious or cultural value to many of the fundamental forms of space and time. According to this belief system, the basic patterns of existence are perceived as sacred because in contemplating them one is contemplating the origin of all things.* "[28] Simply, it's about mathematics, signs, symbols, phi and Fibonacci theorems. It's way over my head but we see it everyday in nature and creation. There are many, many crop circles, for example, that show us sacred geometry. I believe these signs and symbols are like numbers and codes to help us awaken to who we really are.

Anyway, while lying in bed one night I consciously tapped into this frequency again and found myself in what looked like a large courtyard filled with many people. Everyone was dressed in extravagant costumes and there was a beautiful lady in front of me holding my hand. She also was in costume and was trying to reveal something to me as she wouldn't let go of my hand. All of a sudden she let go and I drifted up above everyone, very much in control of this flight. As soon as she let go of my hand music started playing and everyone started dancing and celebrating.

At first I wondered if this was pagan ritual and I no longer had to be a part of it. What does that mean you ask? I felt as if I no longer had to go back to the ways of this world. There was a new way in a new world. My faith had been tested and I passed the test. This was somewhat refreshing as I know what I had endured up to that point and had fully understood that if I stayed the course there was, metaphorically speaking, a pot of gold at the end of this rainbow.

As I flew above everyone there was a feeling of sadness and despair for the others below. I very much wanted to help but it seemed as if nobody really cared about being caught up in this never-ending ritual. I then flew into what I will call a cube which I had seen at a prior time while studying this geometry. No matter what direction I was facing, regardless if I was upside down or not, I was still feeling right side up. This is hard to describe and the only thing I could come up with is this: If a bug is walking on the ground and comes to the wall he is able to walk up the wall. Now the wall he is walking up is his floor and the adjacent wall is his ceiling. If he continues up the wall and starts walking on the ceiling the floor becomes his ceiling. Don't get me wrong here; I fully understand that in the 3rd density we still have gravity however bugs are able to defy it because of the apparatus on their feet. While in this particular multidimensional cube there was no gravity and no matter in what direction I looked there was a new perception of what I was seeing.

In short, we know of one way to perceive our floors, walls and physical surroundings. We walk on the floor and we recognize that it is the floor. In this particular dimension that I was in, nothing was defined as is. It was like creating as you go along and no matter what you create it is always correct with the inability to create anything wrong. Matter of fact there was nothing wrong. Everything and everywhere was always the correct perception of everything I was experiencing. Sorry I can't give a better analogy as my limited mind has a difficult time explaining something that only lasted a brief period of time as we know it.

After spinning over and over like being in space with no gravity, except everything kept revealing itself as right side up, I popped back into my body. This is the only time I heard the popping sound I told you about earlier. As bizarre as it all sounds this was pretty cool.

PITTSBURGH

One night, in surroundings that seemed very much like Pittsburgh, I found myself sitting in the back of a convertible car like you would in a parade, traveling at a very high speed. I guess I have always had a propensity for that. Once again, sometimes you gotta laugh at yourself! We were racing another car to this bridge that had room for only one vehicle. I never noticed who I was with as I was somewhat frightened because I felt as if someone was going to die very soon.

We entered this bridge at the same time the other car did and I remember everyone laughing. As I told you I was the one sitting up in the back so I knew I was going to die. As soon as we hit the overpass I started to duck only to realize that we went right through it. Everyone was still laughing and I knew that this obviously was my turn to figure out that when you are astral traveling, it is in your etheric body and there is no matter in this body.

As soon as I was shown this reality I was no longer in the car but I kept flying through a building into a huge atrium. I slowed down and could see other people in what was the prettiest atrium I had ever witnessed. I am not quite sure where it was other than, as I said, it seemed like I was in Pittsburgh. As soon as I touched down I snapped back into my body in bed.

I still have no idea who I was with and the learning experience was obviously that we can travel through matter.

CLASSROOM

I will give you one more occasion in the astral realm in the 4th dimension. This astral realm is a different frequency than experiencing the other frequencies in the 4th density. There is the emotional plane, mental plane, spiritual plane and probably others that I cannot define but are nonetheless still in the 4th. If I receive the answers I will give them but rest assured there are others that can give them with enough research. This particular time was probably in the mental or emotional plane as I did not fly. I was out of my physical body but cannot remember flying.

I found myself in what seemed like a classroom with other people and a teacher. I was sitting down and looked up at the clock. All of a sudden the clock started coming out of the wall and I mentally tossed it down to the ground and it splattered all over the floor. Needless to say it got everyone's attention. The feeling that came over me was that time was running out and I got angry. I got up and started trying to throw other things on the ground but my hands went right through them. I approached the teacher and asked her, "Why now?" She told me it was not her call. I then told her that I didn't believe her and was going into the bathroom to look at myself in the mirror. As soon as I got to the bathroom, I could physically turn the light on and as soon as I looked up to the mirror I snapped back into my body in bed.

The feeling of this particular experience was that time is running out and we will have a conscious decision to make in this density of free will as to where we will be going. I am assuming it is the winter solstice in December 2012, a subject still to come. This, friends, I do not know. I don't know why I was angry other than I felt there was unfinished business.

Let me reiterate, these planes of realities or frequencies are very real. These are not dreams although your dreams are nothing more than remembering what your soul is doing in these particular planes. As the veil from the physical realm and the nonphysical realm continues to thin, we will continue to be aware of these realms consciously just as if you wake and live your normal 3D life.

It's important to know that communicating in the etheric realms is done by telepathy. There is no need for talking. Actually, I don't even think it is possible to talk. Again, in the 3rd density we only use 10% of our brains. One thing you must accept is the fact that when you die in the 3rd dimension your brain is made of matter. We perceive our brains as what controls our daily walk. Our brains are for the function of our physical bodies but our soul is what connects us to the mind of God. Therefore, it is paramount that we find out who we are other than the flesh. When you do, these other realms are shown to you.

Morphing and Other Revelations

———————— • ————————

M ORPHING, WHEN A SHAPE SHIFTS or transitions from one form to another, is off the charts in the 4th dimension. People, things, virtually anything of matter can change right before your very eyes. I am not really sure how much emphasis the forces of darkness have in this freaky experience or if it comes mainly from ones own subconscious or what. I haven't found complete answers in my research. All I know is it is real. The scary part of this experience is when you've never seen it before. It will test your manhood. Again, depending on your state of mind at the time, your experience can be turning a bush into a beautiful angel or the most grotesque alien being you can imagine. Unfortunately I experienced most of the latter.

The good part of this experience is learning about reality and the illusion of matter. Matter is an illusion. As mentioned before it is just a lower vibrating form of molecules that form our world. All that is required for us humans to stick our hand through the wall is for the wall's vibration to rise or for us to raise our vibration and voila, you got it. Just like the way morphing works, matter can and does change when frequency changes.

I once did a school report on tornadoes, which were a part of my life because I grew up in Kansas right in the middle of Tornado Alley. I found out that in these tornadoes the electromagnetic energy caused straw to permeate glass without breaking the glass. They somehow formed together without any damage. There are many other similar scenarios about matter permeating matter. I know we have all heard the phrase, mind over matter. Put your mind to work because it's an amazing tool.

There really are many people out there who have the ability to move matter, bend spoons and do whatever they put their minds to. There is a story about a man in India who has the ability to physically manifest jewelry and such items out of thin air, which he gives to the poor people. There is also a story about a guy who, through machines, sends certain waves through metal and you can visually watch it melt.

As I mentioned earlier, this stuff never really spooked me. Maybe this is one of the reasons I have been able to experience what I have. I can certainly guarantee you that once you have pierced the veil into other realms, watching someone bend a spoon will seem quite boring. Don't get me wrong, I have tried to accomplish this and cannot do it for whatever reason, but I still feel that I will be capable of it.

I know you are thinking this is all very drastic, but like I said it only takes one time of raising your consciousness higher and then you will have a great perception of how these things are possible.

Communicating with Nature

———————•———————

THE ABILITY TO COMMUNICATE WITH NATURE goes way back in time. Here in the Western hemisphere it is really not understood but is catching on. There are, however, some people that have this ability and are quite adept. Some people are hired to communicate with animals just as if you would send a member of your family to the doctor or psychiatrist. Television programs, movies and books portray people who are believed to have great communicative powers with dogs or horses, for example, and to understand them intuitively.

I went through a period of approximately two weeks where I could communicate intuitively with animals, birds, reptiles, trees and probably anything that I put my mind to at the time. I actually testified to this ability in court, which as you might imagine didn't fly too well. I really didn't care what the other people in the courtroom thought; especially for the fact that I thought they were trying to make me look crazy. I felt like all of the inhabitants in the room didn't care one damn bit about my well-being.

One thing I couldn't understand was that the unbelievers were also the professing Christians who believed in the wonderful stories in the Bible about Jonah living in the mouth of the whale for three days, the turning of water into wine and three guys being thrown into a fiery furnace and coming out unscathed. They believed these and many more, and were then criticizing me. I state that I can communicate with nature and that's unacceptable?

We have the ability to communicate with everything that has a consciousness, whether that communication is by our form of speech or something else. We primarily communicate with one another with the five senses that are provided to us while living the 3D experience. Not everyone though, as some have supernatural communication skills they possess and use. We all do, we just haven't used them in so long we have forgotten how to access them. We are starting to awaken to this ability.

Have you ever wondered how animals or insects communicate? How about twins who, without talking to each other, know what is happening to their sibling?

Have you ever seen the movie *The Matrix?*[29] Whether you are aware of it or not we do live in a matrix. These grids are everywhere and both consciousness and communication travel throughout the grids.

There are different grids of vibration that animals and insects use that are at a different vibration level from human communication. Once again, if you change your vibration you can tap into this grid. Find it bizarre? Well the same scenario applies to plants and trees, because remember that they have a consciousness too.

There is much to learn about in this world we live in. As long as we continue to deny our capabilities, or should I say deny God's capabilities, we will continue coming back to the 3rd dimension.

I find it amusing as well as saddening, when I see people who walk around this 3rd dimension acting like they own it and thinking they are more superior to others, because of wealth or intelligence. I will correlate this intelligence to ego. If you think that you have mastered this life in this dimension and perceive yourself as superior to others, or that your religion is better than the rest, please write a book and let the rest of us know the secret to your success.

I am very aware of what you cannot do. Show me what you can do and then teach me how to do it because I want it all, all the time.

Don't ridicule me because I can do some things that you can't. I can tell you that you can do the very same things, but only you can decide to do it.

Time Travel

———————— • ————————

HAVE YOU EVER READ THE BOOK OR SEEN the movie *The Philadelphia Experiment*? According to the story that is told in the movie, our military and the powers-that-be had under their control a group of brilliant scientists who had knowledge of how to travel back and forth through time.[30]

The proposed plan was for the military to obtain the capability of making a ship disappear, thus adding a very powerful weapon to their arsenal. These particular scientists had the knowledge of quantum physics, electromagnetism, energy fields and whatever else was involved for this to happen. They built a machine and were going to test it on The USS Eldridge while the ship was sitting in Philadelphia Harbor. When they cranked their machine on, the ship allegedly disappeared and was teleported to the harbor in Norfolk, Virginia and back again to the Philadelphia Naval Shipyard.

The experiment went haywire and the people aboard during the experiment were mentally screwed up. They supposedly were able to break through the space-time continuum and Mother Nature assured them that what they were doing was definitely butter and not "Parkay." The U.S. Navy denies that the experiment ever took place and you probably won't find any information on this experiment to confirm that it did, in fact, exist.[31]

Many years ago I was able to get my hands on some underground information concerning this event but I am not here to confirm one way or the other whether or not this story about traveling through time is fact or fiction.

What I am here to tell you, however, is that time travel is real and it happens all the time. To take it one step further there is no such thing as time because time is an illusion. We may believe we experience time in 3D in a linear fashion, in a logical sequence of events, but this is also an illusion. Great philosophical minds have long debated the concept of time and the illusion of time.

One day while walking down the beach I decided to go see some friends at a nearby condominium. I went to the north side of their building and pressed the button for the guard to let me in. He did and I went up to their door only to find them gone, so I went downstairs and walked out of the south side of the building. I got about ten feet outside the door and was immediately teleported to the other side of the building where I had been approximately ten minutes before.

What would you do if that happened to you? I have to tell you at the time of this experience I was still very green to all of these phenomena that were occurring. This really blew my mind but I wanted to do it again. After calming down and making sure that what I just experienced really happened I proceeded to the other side of the building. I was going to retrace my steps in hopes that it would happen again. I tried everything but to no avail.

Again, I cannot tell you why I've experienced these things other than to tell you about our divinity. I cannot consciously perform these feats at will but I can convey to you in laymen's terms how they happened.

I have had experiences where it seems as if everything around me is pulsating at one beat and the feeling is of being in heaven. When these incidents happen to me I get a very prominent feeling there is no such thing as time. And I can tell you there is no such thing as time in the spiritual realms. In the 3rd dimension, because everything is vibrating at a slower rate than the speed of light, we have a built-in clock from our creator for this experience down here. This is called linear time as our daily lives are measured in past, present and future. This is actually another illusion of reality on this side of the veil.

When I experienced everything communicating the same thought there was no time. I know this is difficult to comprehend, as your mind is not trained yet to realize this truth. On this side of the veil we interpret past, present and future. In the higher frequencies there is no illusion of this feeling, only the now.

If you are in Los Angeles and travel east by plane and go all the way around the world until you get back to Los Angeles you will have experienced 24 hours of linear time in the space that you covered. If you take a space ship up into space and look back at a very small Earth you can actually visualize the 24-hour trip you just took all in one moment.

I mentioned about seeing my family, friends and even myself on the beach, in other planes of reality. Did I witness them in the past, present or future? I am positive that I was shown my parents and brother 40 years younger to prove this truth that time is an illusion. So the next time you are in a hurry, step back and realize that the only important thing in our lives is right now. Live every moment to the fullest because you certainly are fooling yourself if you are planning for something that is really nothing but an illusion.

Warfare in the Spiritual Realm

———————— • ————————

THE 4ᵀᴴ DIMENSION, AS I EXPLAINED EARLIER, is where the battle between dark and light, good and evil occurs. It is the spiritual battleground and I have many stories concerning warfare in the spiritual realms.

I will share an experience I had while consciously in the 4ᵗʰ dimension. At the time I was trying to apply this strange new world to the Bible and definitely was looking for some answers. I was going through some serious spiritual warfare and needed some things explained.

One day while studying the numbers 666 and the color red, both of which are used in references to Satan, I decided to take a walk and go to eat lunch. While walking along the road I noticed that traffic had picked up going both ways. As far as I could see it was bumper to bumper with the cars traveling approximately 45 mph. This was like Sunday beach traffic but at a time of year when there is none. More importantly, the cars were traveling way too fast.

Whenever you consciously tap into these other realms you must understand that you aren't going to another planet. All of your surroundings are familiar and you are in the same place except you will probably *feel* like you are literally in another world. The cool thing about entering these planes is whatever is most prominent in your mind is what will automatically be manifested. The scary thing is if you're having a bad day then you will manifest bad things. Still pretty cool but when you're new at the game you can't figure out how all of this stuff in your mind immediately shows up in front of you.

I couldn't believe how thick this traffic was and started trying to figure out why. I then noticed that, going both ways for as far as I could see, every sixth car was the color red. I had to walk about a mile to the restaurant and this sight never changed. I actually called my parents in Kansas to figure out if I was still in this world. They answered the phone which really didn't help my dilemma. I started thinking to myself, what are the mathematical odds of something like this happening? It would be hundreds of times easier to win the lottery than for something like this to happen. In the 3rd dimension it absolutely, unequivocally isn't possible.

I had walked near the road to see if this was actually real. I could feel the wind and hear the cars so I decided against stepping out into traffic. This was one of many experiences with spiritual warfare in the 4th dimension and was definitely a mind freak.

One never engages in real spiritual warfare until they pierce the veil into the spiritual arena. There is a book written by Watchman Nee called *Spiritual Man* that has a great statement about spiritual warfare. Spiritual warfare is not a physical battle but one that is fought with the spirit, in the mind. Until a Christian has experienced the baptism of the Holy Spirit, he or she cannot truly understand and enter the spiritual world, according to Nee. It is necessary to gain "revelation in his spirit." [32]

When someone has entered this world, the real difficulties will begin. "This is the period where the power of darkness disguises itself as an angel of light and even attempts to counterfeit the Person and the work of the Holy Spirit. It is also the moment when the intuition is made aware of the existence of a spiritual domain and of the reality of Satan and his evil spirits."[33] The trials now put on this person may be emotional ones, or involve situational factors. The believer's environment may be unsettled and their efforts and works may be blocked.

Because the battle is a spiritual one, the "weapons" are spiritual as well. The battles are not fought with arms of the flesh. "It is the struggle between the spirit of man and that of the enemy, an engagement of spirit vs. spirit." Gaining the knowledge of, and strength in, the Holy Spirit to win this battle is not something accomplished at one time. Instead it happens gradually, as the person more fully understands the reality of Satan and his kingdom.[34]

This warfare I experienced was undoubtedly the most difficult task I have ever encountered. For me personally, the *Book of Job* had great relevance, as there really is no consolation from anyone or anything. It's like the Lord telling Satan, "Do whatever you want but do not take his life."[35] This warfare has no comparison. For me it was all about the mind. I honestly would have accepted any physical pain to give relief to my mind. I have endured plenty of physical pain in my life and learned how to adapt, but the mind war was excruciating.

Once you experience baptism in the Holy Spirit and connect with the mind of God your intuition will be your compass from that point forward. You will not want to leave it for one hour of any day. There will always be the constant connection that you can rely on.

Once in the spiritual realms there is a difference between experiencing something supernatural and something God wants to reveal to you. If your soul is supposed to experience spiritual warfare then you will no doubt experience both.

It is interesting when I hear lifelong professing Christians comment about spirituality and demonic activity from books they have read or stories they have been told. My opinion on this is if you haven't experienced the warfare in the spiritual realms then you really don't understand the magnitude of the war.

There is a reason you are allowed into the spiritual realms, however, Satan, "The Prince of the Power of the Air"[36] also understands your accomplishment. He will disguise himself of light and you will no doubt experience plenty of phenomena that will blow you away. Respect this as it is. Remember, it's all an illusion. The things you will consciously see will be like walking through the desert for many days and visualizing a city up ahead. Once you get to what you saw, it turns out to be nothing so you look up again only to notice another city far off into the distance. The illusion in the heat waves is a metaphor of the reality we see in the 3rd dimension. We just haven't figured it out yet. The dark forces understand the illusion of our reality and will no doubt play tricks on the mind. However, they must reap what they sow. This universal law is a constant.

Vibration is the universal language of the spirit. I might need to explain a little more about vibration and piercing the veil into the spiritual realms. Remember, like attracts like when it comes to vibration. It's easy to be confused as to how you "tap in" yet still live in 3D. At my current level of ascension I'm not like the character in the television show "Bewitched"[37] where I can twitch my nose and tap into another realm. This process doesn't work like that, at least not yet; eventually we all will be able to. As your consciousness rises in vibration you are consciously able to tap into these other frequencies. Remember, this world and all of these other worlds are nothing more than different frequencies that are interpreted by our minds. The way we were created—our bodies, minds, electromagnetism, quantum physics and many other criteria that I can't even explain - make it possible for this amazing show to take place.

Personally, I don't believe I've ever consciously said to myself, "All right, I am going to raise my level of consciousness and slip into the 4th dimension." It just happens. I could be anywhere at any time and it just happens. Make no mistake, when it does there is no denying it. You actually feel the difference and sense the difference even though the surroundings can be the same.

There will be other times when you slip in and feel completely different sensations. I am assuming that at these times they are higher dimensions from the 5th on. The 5th dimension in most religions is referred to as Heaven. There are some great references concerning these other realms. Go online or to a bookstore and go into the metaphysical section, there is plenty of information on everything in this book. You'll quickly discover that I'm not the only believer out here!

I have many stories of the spiritual warfare that can be discussed at a further date. These stories are so bizarre that it's probably better to refrain from telling them now. I have a website that might be a better forum. I would rather someone ask me about something they are struggling with and I will be happy to explain other scenarios. I really don't want to spook anyone, as most of this stuff is already hard enough to digest. One suggestion though, please do not discount any of this information because I honestly expect everyone will be experiencing ascension in one way or another and it will be instructive.

One must realize spiritual warfare is what it is: *spiritual* warfare. It doesn't take place in this plane of existence. It takes place in the spiritual realm, plain and simple. If you have two flat tires in one day and think you are going through spiritual warfare I've got some waterfront property in Arizona to sell you.

5.

"In my Father's house are many mansions: if it were not so, I would have told you. I go to prepare a place for you."

John 14:2

Heaven on Earth

———————————— • ————————————

E VEN THOUGH THERE ARE PLENTY OF frightening things in
the fourth density, the wonderful things there and
beyond are what we should be striving to achieve. These are the
miracles that we read about in the Bible. I don't believe there is any
more duality in the realms after the 4th dimension. My experiences
lead me to believe these higher realms are of unity and oneness with
no separation. I only wish everyone could experience this
immediately to realize that we are all the same. Everything is the
same. I don't care if you are a dirt clod on Mars, an insect or a
person here on earth. You would fully understand that everything
in existence has the same building blocks of creation in it whether
visible or invisible. I guarantee you would care less about who is
doing steroids or picking their nose. You would however feel a
complete humbleness and awe for our creator.

One time while playing pool at night I slipped into a higher realm than the 4th. I'm not sure how high up the ladder I was but I'm assuming this was in the 5th plane or higher. Everything in the place started vibrating at the same pulse and there was a feeling of warmth and pure love that came over me. All of the colors were enhanced ten-fold. It looked like everything turned to neon. This was one of these experiences I spoke of earlier. It was totally awesome. I could hear the music from the other room as well as my friends talking across the room. The incredible thing about this was everything that was going through my mind was exactly the same as the song that was playing and the conversation my friends were having.

This can be explained because when we move higher and get closer to source we start experiencing that everything is the same. Everything comes from the mind of God and therefore *is* the mind of God! You can actually feel the pulse of God in everything and there is complete unison in everything. The clarity of it all is beyond our imagination here. Can you envision going to a club and everyone's conversation in there is communicating the same thought? I know you can't. It cannot be comprehended by our non-awakened minds.

This sensation, which I will declare is the closest to God that I've ever been, has only happened one other time when I was sitting one day as a passenger in rush hour traffic. Again, everything, every sound, didn't matter. If it was a bus engine or a car radio, or the pavement; everything pulsed to the same vibration. Everything was pure love, all on the same path back to source because everything was receiving the same energy from God.

Remember when you first fell in love with your significant other and you had that warm fuzzy feeling inside. It didn't matter what was going on in the world, all you wanted was the other person and for that feeling to continue forever. It's like this. As the feeling takes over your body the colors and clarity explode. It's almost as if everything turns to pure crystal. The thing you feel is that overwhelming sensation of love, multiplied by ten.

I really learned at that very moment in traffic how everything is alive. I know this is something most do not realize but you must understand this. Everything has the building blocks of creation in it. Everything has a consciousness. We are different in the fact that we have a spirit and soul but please understand the ground you walk on is a living organism, just as everything is.

This was a serious changing point in my life as I came to respect creation and nature. I started applying what I experienced to the things that I have done throughout my life that were disrupting the flow of nature. I mentioned earlier about personally suffering through some things in my life that I didn't think were justified. I started receiving answers to all of the things I went through and why they happened. The results were karma.

If you go through your life and disrupt the harmonic flow of creation it will come back to you at some point. It is universal law. If you learn anything from this book please know this as truth. The new world is one where the lion lays down with the lamb. There won't be any killing or destruction. Everyone will accept everyone and everything as they are, a living entity created for a specific purpose from the mind of God. (Isaiah 11:6-9, RSV)

Again, this is something that we presently cannot comprehend in this dimension because this dimension consists of duality, polarity, contrast, separation, war, peace and every similar equation.

In this realm our greatest achievements arrive from a dual or a battle. Our greatest heroes are the very people that had to overcome a foe, or win a championship. We are judged on our accomplishments. We are also judged on the amount of money we make and I will say it again, money is wonderful. It allows for a lot of nice things and certainly takes care of a lot of problems. The paradox of this realm is it is fleeting and it is an illusion. Like I said earlier, all that is required to stick your hand through matter is to raise your level of vibration.

In the higher realms we won't have to experience this. Everything you desire is automatically at your disposal. Whatever you think automatically appears. Everything is one with no duality and no separation. It's like a constant stream of Nirvana. Can you imagine this?

Everything is Connected

———— • ————

A S WE RAISE OUR LEVEL OF CONSCIOUSNESS and actually get closer to source we start to experience more fully how everything is connected. In the 3rd dimension where we experience separation, polarities and duality, we envision others as separate from ourselves. For the most part we feel much closer to our immediate family members because we have something in common with them in the flesh. As we raise our level of consciousness and this feeling of separation diminishes, we will actually feel more in tune with all of our surroundings and start accepting others as they are regardless of their lifestyles.

One difficulty we have in this reality is we feel separated from God as well. Even our prayers seem to be directed towards someone or something up there or out there somewhere. This feeling will change also, with the realization that God is in everything. We have been taught that God is either a gray-haired, older white man in a robe or a white man that looks like Jesus. If your skin color is anything other than white, you may have felt this scenario to be a little peculiar.

We were made in the image of God, which is spirit. When you pierce the veil into the spiritual realms the connection to God and everything in creation is very prevalent. In the 3rd dimension part of the illusion is feeling separation, but in the higher realms we are very much connected to our creator at all times.

One day while out on the dock listening to the radio, I was given another opportunity to realize how everything is connected. This happens and none of it will be premeditated, it just happens.

I was listening to a football game and my level of consciousness rose and I was able to tap in again. I was stretching my knees as I often do. As I squatted down I accidentally fell back. At the moment I fell back the commentator announcing the game said the quarterback was falling back. I moved my hand through the air and at the same time he said the ball was moving through the air. I stood up and he stated that the play call was going to stand up. This went on for a few minutes and everything I did was exactly duplicated by this commentator on the air. Again, everything in the higher realms is absolutely, unequivocally connected. It is here, but it is not experienced.

At this point in my quickening this kind of experience is very prominent in my daily walk. This is a really neat environment to live in as you feel like a character in a movie except you are the one writing the script as you go along. The difficult thing to comprehend is that we are all making up our script. We are the ones creating the world we live in moment by moment.

As you grow in this process, these synchronicities will continue to manifest more and more. You can be listening to the television and reading a book at the same time and the person on TV will say a word and you will read the exact same word in your book at the exact same moment. People who are unaware of this phenomenon will say that it is an incredible coincidence but there is no such thing as coincidence in our lives. Everyone and everything is connected and these synchronicities happen to awaken you to this reality.

Your thoughts are constantly affecting the quality of your happiness. Regardless of the things that happen to us, the way we feel at the time is the reality we create for ourselves. There is no way to avoid the negative things that pop up in our lives. The important thing is our reaction to them. Either the glass is half empty or half full. Just allow everything to be. Allow everything to remain in constant motion and change, whether you are aware of the changes or not.

Mass consciousness is changing. I can tell by the movies and shows that are presented to the public. The connection of what is above is as below will be noticed as you ascend.

Reincarnation

———————•———————

THE MOST IMPORTANT PART OF THIS GAME down here is waking up to the fact that you personally have been in control of every minute of your own life since inception. Sound strange? I keep telling you, truth is stranger than fiction.

There are no victims in this world. If there were the game would be flawed. If "Joey the Fish" is killing people every other month, rolling in the dough and living in a mansion while "The Beaver" is working his rear end off struggling to pay the bills and going to church every Sunday, which one is going to heaven when they die? Our Heavenly Father loves us all the same and he wants everyone in heaven. You remember the story in the Bible about the lost Sheep.[38] He doesn't leave anyone!

This is where reincarnation comes in and oh, by the way there are different levels of what we consider hell, but it is of your own creation. Believe me you can create the most miserable hell imaginable for your soul to experience. The good thing is you don't have to stay. You can leave that reality whenever you choose; it's all up to you. Our creator hasn't anything to do with what negativity you choose to create upon yourself. Did you forget that you, yes, you are a co-creator. Yes, it's in the Good Book.

To me, the belief that I was born, grew up and will either go to Heaven or Hell is way worse than believing in Santa Claus, the Easter Bunny and the Tooth Fairy. I don't believe we die and then spend eternity in one or the other reality. I believe there are many realities and billions of galaxies that are continuing to evolve. Jesus said, "In my Father's house are many mansions."[39] These mansions are not big homes on a hill in a place called Heaven. They are the many different dimensions that we have the ability to experience.

Back to Joey the Fish and the Beaver. This is where the gift of mercy comes in concerning all of these different souls out there who all come from the same source but yet are all different. The gift of mercy is reincarnation. It's in the Bible, although this has been a stumbling block for Christianity from inception.

If Joey the Fish has spent a lifetime treating everyone horribly he's not allowed in the Kingdom. That we all agree on. What about the Beaver though, he lived a wonderful harmonious life. Is he allowed in? I believe this depends on many variables that unfortunately I cannot give answers to.

I believe that the major part of being a mature soul is ridding one's self of the karmic wheel. This would entail going through many lifetimes in this density with the ability to figure the game out and dumping many lifetimes of negative energy.

However, I am a believer in what a lot of people have written about which is when we physically pass on from this density, i.e. die, we are taken up to what I will call "summer vacation." This is a place where you will meet up with others in your soul family as well as your guides and then discuss what and where is the next place for your soul to go to continue your journey.

If the best choice for the maturity of your soul is to reincarnate on earth, then you will have parents, brothers, sisters and others picked out for you before coming down. Your problem in the previous life might be your destiny on return. Or, if you were a man, you might return as a woman, and vice versa. There is no doubt in my mind that all of us have been male and female many times over.

I mentioned earlier that there are no victims and I mean it. We have man-made laws and there are spiritual laws that we must adhere to. There is no way around them. Just like we are given the gift of reincarnation until we 'get it right.'

The universal law of karma allows the world to be free of victimization. We reap what we sow. This is something I wasn't aware of until there were things that happened to me that I didn't feel were warranted. I did some searching and the voice inside informed me of this energy thing that has to even itself out before you are allowed to move on. Remember the number 11:11 awakening and everything in the world going back to zero balance.

If you are carrying some karmic tickets you are, unfortunately, going to have to cash them in. The surprising thing is that you might not have accumulated them in this life. This could be negative energy that your soul has brought with it.

The most important thing for you to do now is stop accumulating them. Stop sending out negative energy because it's going to come back, folks. Every thought that pops into your mind is very powerful energy that is sent out on the matrix and universal law demands that it find a home. You will receive what you send. Why do you think the Bible says if you think of a sin, then you have already committed it? The minute it is thought of, that energy goes out on the grids.

I can assure you whatever it is that is a pain in your behind at the present moment in life is exactly what you came around again to work on. I can tell you that you are God incarnate just like Jesus said two thousand years ago and that everything you need is right inside you, but you won't believe me. But yet when it comes to judging others like a God we are all for that. We don't know anything about ourselves but we seem to know a lot about everyone else. Give it some effort, I promise you when you really find yourself you won't be interested in judging others.

The Mayan Calendar

—————— • ——————

IF THERE WAS ONE TOPIC THAT BROUGHT out the critic in people when I started to talk about it, this was the one. You might have thought from reading some comments that I alone invented this and I was making dire predictions about the future of humankind. Not quite.

Let me explain. The ancient Maya Civilization lived in the areas that are now several countries in Central America and certain regions of southern Mexico. Considered an advanced culture, they flourished in these areas over 2,000 years ago. The Maya were very adept at mathematics and astronomy and were in tune with the different ages and the evolution of consciousness from age to age.

They developed and used several complex calendars using astronomical elements including the cycles of the moon and sun and the movements of the planets. One of these, called the "Long Count" calendar, is widely believed to be a prophetic calendar. The end of this dispensation of time, according to the calendar, is December 21, 2012.[40] Some people have referred to this date as Doomsday or the end of the world.[41] One reason given is because on that date it is predicted that an astronomical event will occur that will have "the sun and earth in alignment with the center of the Milky Way Galaxy and the earth will wobble on its axis." Apparently, this only happens every 26,000 years.[42]

Some writers, based on their insecurities and egos, have incorrectly said, "I believe it will be the end of the world." It's an interesting thought to ponder, but not true. I do not believe the Mayan Calendar is the prediction of the end of the world.

Rather I, like many others, believe that this date has significance for the spiritual awakening of the masses – all of us. The Mayans predicted that consciously we will be entering what they termed as The Golden Age. I firmly agree, as things and people are already moving in that direction. I project that almost everyone will be experiencing the phenomena written in this book in the near future.

December 21, 2012 signifies the start of a new era, a new reality if you will. This is the dawning of the Age of Aquarius that people have spoken of. This means there will be a new time when everyone's level of consciousness will be raised. Some say this date will be the end of cycles of time in the history of the world. One commentator, Janae Weinhold on her website writes, "It is a moment when humanity, Planet Earth, the Milky Way Galaxy and perhaps all of creation is expected to take a simultaneous leap in evolution." [43]

This event has been prophesized by many cultures, tribes and religions. This, in my mind is an event that we should want. If this is a profound change in peoples' hearts, minds and souls then I'm all for it. I've seen enough of what we have created in this current dispensation. Aren't you tired of fighting? Do we really honestly know what we are fighting for, or do we just accept what they tell us? The voice inside me tells something very, very different than what I am receiving on the television, radio or in the papers.

People who have no understanding of this typically are led by their egos once again and have to force out some ignorant statement or article in hopes of making this seem very ridiculous. This is and has been the primary reason we as a society fail to learn anything. We are programmed to learn what Big Brother wants us to learn and anything beyond that is fallacy.

The reason that people are unaware of this prophetic calendar and what is taking place is we no longer spend enough time looking up like they did in the old days. We are inundated with the daily grind in the 3rd dimension. I have my views and opinions as to how all of this transpired and I see my job as helping to get you started. If you ever feel compelled to find out what happened to our Garden of Eden and society in itself, there is plenty of material out there concerning this. Let's first get you believing in you and your awesome powers and then go after the real crazy stuff.

There are some amazing things going on in our solar system at this moment in history that leaves science very perplexed. As I mentioned earlier, time is speeding up whether you are aware of it or not. I am and have noticed it for a while. The sensitives seem to be very well connected as to what is taking place.

All of these events have been prophesized; what is above is as below. Everything is connected and our Father will not allow us to experience this shift without us having knowledge of it. Trust me in that there will be many skeptics out there concerning this information. Such is the beauty of free will.

As we get closer to 2012, I feel that everything will be escalated, whether it's your perception of things negative or positive. It really is your choice how to get through this shift. I do believe the symptoms described earlier are things that might be unavoidable concerning Mother Earth and all of her inhabitants. We are definitely changing.

Extraterrestrials

———————— • ————————

M OST OFTEN WHEN CONVERSATION is about metaphysics people automatically correlate that to believing in aliens. I'm not quite sure what they mean when they say aliens. I will assume that they are referring to beings that live on other planets foreign to this one we reside on. I had never understood the big dilemma related to this subject even before seeing other people in other dimensions.

Let's see, we currently live on a planet called Earth. Our astronomers tell us that we are one planet out of many in our solar system and that there are also billions of other galaxies out there. Well let me ponder this one without my ego telling me that I'm the greatest and this so-called God of mine made all of this just for me and my friends on this little rock third out from the sun.

We really don't even know who we are, so how in the heck can we even remotely comment on something we really don't know anything about? Maybe it's that all-knowing ego again. Seriously, think about this for a moment. Where did we actually learn if there are or are not aliens out there? I believe we were told by someone along the line that there isn't such a thing. We really don't need to bring up the Roswell incident, Area 51 and all of the alleged underground facilities. We already know that those stories are all untrue, because "they" told us they were untrue.

Well, who told us and why do we have to agree?

Why are people chastised about a particular belief in something that mainstream society disagrees with? Are we stupid or is it our egos, because if you really want us to believe in something all you have to do is inundate us with it and our mass consciousness will make it reality.

Hopefully you will get inundated with the truth about a lot of things and be able to form your own opinion about them. So what if you have a different opinion than the rest of society - you are probably right. The rest of society does what they are told to do and they do it because they certainly do not want to be considered different.

I can tell you that I am aware of over 6 billion "aliens" and they currently live on planet Earth, at least in this reality in the 3rd dimension. Most of them think that because they were born here, this is where they come from. Folks, you are spiritual beings that chose to experience this reality on this planet but I assure you that you didn't start here. Therefore you are these "aliens."

There are 4th dimensional and higher beings that at times you can see. Please don't be shocked when the others start showing up. I can only inform you that the only reason you can't see them is because we're on different frequencies. Either they have lowered their frequency or you have raised yours. As uncomfortable as it is for us to ascend to grow into our light bodies it is uncomfortable for other ascended beings to lower their frequencies into our density.

There is a simple way to equate a lot of things in our lives and to answer some of the questions that you are presented with but you must first get rid of your fears and insecurities. Most people try and apply logic to the only reality they know, which is 3D. We apply every single one of our questions and answers to 3rd dimensional construct. Herein lays the problem of obtaining knowledge and wisdom. You can only obtain so much knowledge and wisdom from a fleshly 3rd dimensional mind. Hence most mysteries in the Bible have and will remain mysteries until one is able to apply them from a spiritual construct, keeping in mind that we are spiritual beings first.

It tickles me when they bring in these so-called experts to deny the ability of our creator. To these experts I say, go back home and climb in under the covers until your fear subsides. It's written all over your face that you are scared to death of something.

It's all out there for you. He's thrown more stuff at us but we continue to doubt him. When you are able to raise your level of consciousness you will be able to see how inundated we are with the signs and symbols of what is going to be revealed next. You will realize how silly our fears and insecurities are and the fact that they really do not "matter" because matter is an illusion. This is virtual reality and again, truth is stranger than fiction.

As mentioned earlier, I perceive there to be a mathematical equation to everything created, even your thoughts. I also discussed that our creator used sacred geometry. Has anybody ever seen a crop circle? You can go online and view all of these crop circles that are all over the world. These are sacred geometry in the finest form. (Yea, I know. Two older men with some stakes and string are making them. I've heard that before!)

These signs and symbols are part of our awakening, just as numbers and codes are very significant. This sacred geometry is around you at all times, you just have not ever learned about it. It's funny that our children are not being taught this information in our school systems. I find that it's an important learning skill.

Someday we will start applying our brilliant minds, not our egos, and think outside of the 3D construct and maybe realize the uniqueness of the different races of human beings living together here on Earth. Maybe we will look at each other and wonder how is it possible that there are different races? After all, we have one God! What happened?

You don't suppose it's like this on other planets do you? Can't be, because I'm going to live my 75 years on Earth and then I get to go to either heaven or hell. I really have no idea what he was thinking when he made all of those other planets—what a waste of time and energy. At least we know one thing for sure...we are the only beings that he created because "they" told me so.

6.

"If then you were raised with Christ, seek those things which are above, where Christ is, sitting at the right hand of God. Set your mind on things above, not on things on the earth."

Colossians 3:1-2

What We Know and Where We are Going

———————●———————

WE KNOW THAT TIMES ARE CHANGING. The sensitives are very much aware of this and are here to inform the masses. These people are modern day prophets who are given information just like prophets of old. They can give you information and advice on how to adjust to these changes but ultimately it is up to you as it is your life, your soul and your destiny. Only you control it.

Times are definitely changing. I remember growing up and playing outside all day long. I really couldn't stand to come inside, even to eat. Now, kids have many other indoor opportunities with video games, computers, and all kinds of technologies to spend their time on. I laugh when I hear about virtual reality games as we are living in virtual reality but aren't aware of it. It's all about the mind now. We are waking up to the fact that reality comes from the mind.

I have told you that everything you need lies deep inside you so learn to listen to that inner voice. That voice is you. It's your soul talking to you and he has been around the block a few times and has bought the shirt. The best compass that you can carry is your intuition. Everyone has experienced guidance from their intuition at one time or another. Remember walking into a room and having the feeling to leave immediately come over you? This is your soul telling you it's time to get the hell out of there.

Your soul is also a great barometer when it comes to measuring positive and negative energy. Sometimes the energy in some places is unbearable to be around—that's why you leave and tell others you really didn't like that place. Like attracts like and if one of your friends says they loved the place, more than likely you guys aren't as close as you thought.

If you have a propensity to get angry and feel that you are a victim then you probably need to reassess your values. Remember that you always have been and always will be in control of your destiny. If someone screwed you over it was planned for your growth and rebalancing of energy. Please don't get me wrong, those who have a propensity to screw others or have a vindictive habit will no doubt get the same in return.

We have learned that reality is really consciousness. Everything we see and feel comes from our consciousness. Our DNA is consciousness and is in the process of changing from 2 strands back to 12. Our metamorphosis includes very specific biological and biochemical changes, in addition to our DNA, in our cells, blood, endocrine system and brain which will affect the energy of the body throughout the dimensional planes. These changes are all taking place on a subatomic, molecular level.

We know we must release our worldly desires, realizing that there is much more to us than our three dimensional lives. I chuckle when I think of the movie Jim Carey starred in several years ago called *The Truman Show* [44] (True-Man Show). If you haven't seen it I won't spoil it for you but it's about a guy who lives in a bubble all of his life not knowing any more about reality other than what he has seen inside the bubble. Kind of makes you think that the powers that are in 3D are poking fun at us because there are a lot of movies and shows that present to us how reality is but we don't believe.

Ascension is actually our level of consciousness that is leaving one dimension and going to another. Through this process we have to go through a lot of emotional clearing. We are required to go through experiences that bring up our fears, insecurities, anger and other emotions that must be dumped.

It is my understanding that these feelings and experiences start in our emotional body and then are felt in our physical body, hence all of the symptoms I described. As we rid our bodies our DNA takes on more light, changing it to a crystalline state that in turn holds our new level of consciousness.

There is no doubt that everyone will have his or her own trials and tribulations to unload once awakened as the changes of reality are very taxing on the mind and the body. Do not be discouraged, you can and will get through it. It is wonderful on the other side.

There are plenty of others who have experienced this process called ascension, awakening, quickening, or whatever you want to label it. There are many that have wonderful abilities beyond our five senses. Please do not be afraid of these gifts as you hold them as well. As we all awaken we realize that we have always had them, we just needed a little help in finding them. Our creator has left no stone unturned and he refuses to leave any of his sheep behind, so enjoy your every moment and respect how wonderful and perfect you are.

I've explained to you how I believe that some are going to and through the 4th dimension to the 5th. Others are not spiritually ready to handle this and will remain consciously in the 3rd dimension. This doesn't mean that some are better than others. I believe everyone will eventually reach an enlightened state on their own time. I do believe we are co-creators and have the ability to change mass consciousness sooner than later but WE ALL HAVE TO WAKE UP!

As the Mayan "Long Count" calendar winds down to 0.0.0.0.0. on December 21, 2012 there will be much revelation of whom and what we are. The numbers go to zero and consciousness, as we know it, will be forever changed. We will collectively create the level of consciousness.

We've learned how the movie *The Matrix* [45] has relevancy to the reality that the world we live in is all in our mind. There are grids of electromagnetic fields around our planet that, at this very moment, hold our consciousness. We connect through our minds to this frequency, which in turn reveals our reality. Because of the energy (Holy Spirit) that our Bible speaks of in the End Time being poured out upon us, these grids are changing, just as our DNA is changing. Remember, everything seen and unseen has the building blocks of creation in it. Everything will be vibrating at a higher level, which will connect us to a higher frequency that will be a higher level of consciousness. The old way of doing things is rapidly leaving us.

We are very aware of a lot of the man-made laws that we try to adhere to everyday, but I do not believe we are as familiar with the universal laws or spiritual laws that surround us and are a part of us at all times. I guess this is why we feel more like men or women than spiritual beings. I don't believe we feel the immediate impact of the consequences when we deny spiritual laws whereas if you break the speed limit and get pulled over you get a ticket on the spot.

Everything is light and the only difference between things seen and unseen is the level of vibration. Things in the 3rd dimension also vibrate at different levels; water, ice and steam are examples. They all consist of the same component; however they are vibrating at different levels.

We continue to judge one another yet we are told not to "lest you be judged."[46] This one really emphasizes how energy works and the fact that your thoughts are very powerful energy. What you send out must return. We certainly reap what we sow. Sin and forgiveness are 3rd dimensional constructs. They do not apply in the higher planes. There is no such thinking at that level of vibration.

We all have probably experienced Déjà vu, although we didn't know that we are multi-dimensional beings living in a multi-dimensional world and the experience of Déjà vu was actually something we just did in another plane of existence. The good thing about experiencing this phenomenon, other than learning that we are multi-dimensional, is realizing that the veil between the spiritual and physical realms is thinning.

We have allowed our egos to take a rest for awhile and have actually contemplated our existence and the fact that we could have came from the star Orion, the constellation Sirius, the star cluster of The Pleiades or a myriad of the billions of other planets besides Earth. We certainly can have an intelligent view. There might be others out there.

After obtaining some of this information that I wasn't aware of, I came to the conclusion that The Face on Mars,[47] The Giza Pyramids, The Sphinx, Stonehenge and all of these other wonderful artifacts might be here for a reason. For the most part, many people have neglected the knowledge of the constellations and everything else out there that reveals who and what we are. I'm not going to go along with the debunkers this time around. I will form my own opinion.

So now, where are we going? There is plenty of information out there for us about what is taking place. This is not a race; there is no finish line. When all of this was created it was for eternity.

The Bible speaks of a new heaven and a new earth. Has this already happened on another plane of existence? Are we waiting for enough people to awaken so we can go and experience this New Heaven and New Earth? What follows are scriptural references to ascension to help you understand more.[48]

"Put ye not off from the day to day, and from cycle to cycle and eon to eon, in the belief that when ye return to this world ye will exceed in gaining the mysteries, and entering into the Kingdom

of Light. For ye know not when the number of perfected souls shall be filled up, and then will be shut the gates of the Kingdom of Light, and from hence none will be able to come in thereby or any go forth. Strive ye that ye may enter while the call is made, until the number of perfected souls shall be sealed and complete, and the door is shut." (Christ Jesus, The Gospel of the Holy Twelve).

I believe this refers to an exact number of souls who are spiritually ready to ascend into this new earth. Once this happens there will be a veil in place in which ascending and descending cannot occur. This door Jesus refers to is the final separation between the New Earth and the Old Earth.

"For as in the days that were before the flood they were eating and drinking, marrying and giving in marriage, until the day that Noah entered into the Ark, and knew not until the flood came, and took them all away; so shall also the coming of the Son of man be. Then shall two be in the field; the one shall be taken, and the other left. Two women shall be grinding at the mill; the one shall be taken, and the other left. Watch therefore: for ye know not what hour your Lord doth come." (Mathew 24:38-42)[49]

"Nevertheless we, according to his promise, look for new heavens and a new earth, wherein dwelleth righteousness." (2 Peter 3:13)

It is a widely held belief that we only use 10% of our brains. Ponder this for a moment. Why would our creator give us something but deny 90% access to it? He didn't! That would be absurd. You wouldn't do it to your children. We confine ourselves because of ignorance. This is the very reason you can tell someone the actual truth and they still won't believe it. It's like religion; people are going to believe what they have been taught and that's that, period!

The Bible is a wonderful tool no matter how much it has been tampered with. There is plenty of information out there that tells us about the pre-Biblical era. If we have been deceived about our existence get in the back of the line because there is so much we don't know about who and what we are.

Why has there been so much controversy about a book representing a particular religion, whether it is the Koran, Bible or any of the others? No wonder He said He would send the Comforter to reveal things to us and that we wouldn't need the written word. For the last 2000 years religion has largely been a divider of peoples, not a unifier. Substitute spirituality like Jesus taught and maybe we can stop arguing and fighting over who has the best God.

When He asked for us to give him 10% he didn't mean 10% of your bank account. Why would He need your money? He can do whatever He wants not needing your money. He is no dummy folks; He knows exactly what religion is about and how many people have been enlightened through the religious process. I have friends and family who have been attending a religious venue since they were able to walk and they haven't one clue as to what I speak of in this book. One of us isn't learning much folks.

No, He was referring to 10% of your mind. Once you give him the 10% of your mind He flips the switch and you are able to tap into the other 90%. Again, you will be fed milk as a child until you make the commitment for the meat. When you merge your 10% into the other 90% I assure you one revelation of divine experience is way more exhilarating than 1000 Sundays of wine and wafers.

Please do not misunderstand me. I in no way care to judge your religious endeavors, for it doesn't affect me one iota. I believe that a lot of churches practice love and unity and that is a good thing. When it comes to the spiritual teachings of Christ they are somewhat limited. So was I. It is very difficult to teach something that you cannot comprehend; ask the Disciples.

If you aren't learning anything about what's inside of you and how to raise your level of consciousness by using energy and opening up your chakras and experiencing other realms through your third eye then your spiritual growth will remain stagnant. No doubt you will be learning a tremendous amount of religion but nothing spiritual.

Oh, I know the next statement is that I had better test the spirits because I could be deceived. Back at you with that one! If you are applying everything you seem to be learning to this particular experience in the flesh then you had better test the spirits because the comfortable convenience of *"I'm all right, someone's going to come save me"* will keep you in 3D forever. Spirituality is only utilized in the spiritual realms hence the name spirituality. If you aren't experiencing spiritual revelations then it isn't spirituality. Religion is man-made and simply refers to the flesh, not the mind. You are a spiritual being and must start applying spiritual practice and thinking to get back there. Once you open yourself up to the real deal you had better definitely test the spirits because YOU will certainly be tested as to why you were able to make it. If it sounds like a classroom so be it, at the moment most of us are in the 3rd dimension.

Until you are awakened to your divinity it is very difficult to comprehend that you have never done anything wrong. You just have never gained the knowledge and wisdom to understand the classroom we attend in 3D. Your higher self, which was made in the image of God, resides everywhere and was made blameless. This was a metaphor through Christ Jesus that really has never been understood in 3D.

As mentioned earlier, sin and forgiveness are 3rd dimensional constructs. Your higher self residing in the higher planes is unable to sin therefore needs no conception of forgiveness. Everything just is!

We are all in this together. We fell together and eventually will all ascend together each on his or her own time. Accept people for who they are and the experiences each must personally go through. There is no doubt in my mind that we all have experienced every possible scenario that we witness from others. The world is a mirror in and of itself. We are all reflections of each other experiencing every possible thought. Our Creator wanted to experience his creation through all of His soul sparks. We are him therefore we get to experience everything he does.

He feels our pain, sorrow, guilt, fears, everything that is manifested in the lower realms that we consciously experience every single day through our five senses. The really cool thing is we are coming into the age where we can start experiencing beyond our five senses. As this experience of living in 3D is coming to an end we get to experience the other side of the coin.

YOU WILL SEE ALL OF THESE THINGS WHEN YOU BELIEVE IN THEM!

7.

"For we being many are one bread and one body, for we are all partakers of that one bread."

1 Corinthians 10:17

Matthew 22:14
Many Are Called But Few Are Chosen

———————— • ————————

EVERYTHING THAT IS DISCUSSED IN THIS BOOK revolves around this very quote in scriptures from the Book of Matthew in the New Testament.[50] As harsh or direct as I seem to be throughout my story, this passage is what comes to mind and one that I believe reflects the sincerity of what I'm trying to convey.

From my own personal experiences there have been two different scenarios relative to my purpose for writing this book. Trust me I have banged them both around enough to form my opinion. The book of Matthew and others speak of those who are either ready for this spiritually, or those who are given the opportunity and simply cannot handle it and are ultimately turned away or die by the sword.

The Bible speaks of what is above is as below, so what you learn from a literal battle on earth must first be applied to a spiritual battle in the heavens. This is something that we fail to consider mainly because we consciously have not pierced the veil into the higher realms to fully understand how this can be.

My first opinion is that when I entered into the 4th density there was much negativity in my life in the 3rd density, which by now you know is the one we are consciously aware of and wake up to everyday. As I mentioned, the newfound ability to create or manifest every thought will undoubtedly separate the men from the boys. When we pierce the veil and this whole new world opens up to us it can be very frightening. It's like you will be a whole new player in a whole new ball game. How much dirty laundry you have in your laundry basket ultimately determines how long you will be able to stay in the heavenly realms.

Bear with me now because this is the most important aspect you must realize if and when you get the call. We really don't know what is resting in our subconscious minds. We wake everyday and consciously live with all of our fears, insecurities, joys, pleasures and other emotions. If we are afraid of heights we don't go up. If we are afraid of elevators we don't go in them. These are controllable conscious actions that we have built in so that we can, for the most part, manage.

The problem when entering into the 4th dimension is we are able to tap into our subconscious mind and from my personal experiences, it really isn't controllable. There's no stopping it. This gets back to many are called and few are chosen and "If you live by the sword you will inevitably die by the sword."[51] I mentioned how some people take their own lives or create a situation that permits their lives being taken.

The statement that I'm trying to make is, once again, this new world is not somewhere else. As a kid I used to look up at the stars and all of the other planets out there, wondering what they are for and if anyone lives on them. Little did I know that we didn't have to travel billions of light years to experience something or some being beyond our current reality. You don't have to travel to another planet; you simply raise your frequency to a higher level of reality that allows you to do things beyond your five senses. We raise our vibrational frequency and voila, the world comes to us.

You will experience the same things Jesus experienced and revealed to us that we are capable of and would be doing. Remember when he said, "We can perform these miracles and even do greater things than I." [52]

O.K., we're moving ahead, don't lose me here. If and when you enter this reality right here in your same skin and have a lot of negative junk in your subconscious mind, it will be manifested. Remember when I mentioned that I felt as if the whole world was against me? The defense mechanism we turn to is our ego and that is when you will die by the sword if you are unable to handle this bizarre new world. I experienced this on more than one occasion. As a matter of fact, it lasted for months and I did create events where I could have perished.

I am not alone in experiencing these sensations. Drunvalo Melchizedek explained, in his book *The Ancient Secret of the Flower of Life,* [53] that when people enter this realm, unless they are ready or able to experience it, they will bring their fears, hatred, and angers with them. Their fears will manifest, and they will attempt to recreate their old, familiar images to deal with what is happening. This is part of the basic human instinct for survival.

In this powerful new and bizarre world, though, their fears arise and persist. People who have died many years before may appear again and scenes from childhood may be revisited, causing people to fear they are hallucinating.

But the power found in Jesus' words in the biblical verse "Blessed are the meek, for they shall inherit the Earth" (Matthew 5:5 (RSV)) means that if they are "sitting in this new world thinking simple thoughts of love, harmony and peace, trusting in God and yourself, then that is exactly what will manifest" in their world." A harmonious and beautiful world will be manifested and the person will survive. [54]

Thanks, Drunvalo; you couldn't describe what I experienced any better!

This gets back to fully understanding that in our 3rd dimensional thoughts, it takes awhile for everything to manifest in our lives. In the 4th dimensional construct our Father tells us, "Watch therefore, for you know neither the day nor the hour." [55]

As this quickening that Jesus spoke of continues to accelerate, more and more of us will start to awaken. Please don't put thorns around my head, make me carry my own cross and hang me because I am trying to help you. There isn't a doubt in my mind that this is and will happen to all of us. It can be the most wonderful thing you've ever experienced. I have mentioned before that you will realize the players in the game and whom you can go to for help. You will also, which is the reason for all of this, figure out exactly who you are and that this material life is at the bottom of the ladder.

Yes I know that some of you "know-it-alls" who actually have to have physical proof with your minimal 3rd dimensional five senses will remain in the 3rd dimension. That's ok, when enough are awakened the new world grids will hold a new mass consciousness and eventually you will get it. Remember, intelligence and knowledge comes from your brain; wisdom comes from your heart.

If you are a know it all, when you get the call you will manifest exactly all of the fears and doubts of thinking that 'YOU' know it all. God be with you egomaniacs because you are in for a world of hurt!

If you are afraid of heights or drowning, when you get the call, you will automatically find yourself on the tallest building in the world or the deepest ocean. If you have a fear of a lack of money then you will find yourself completely broke out on the street while your wife and kids are wondering what in the hell happened to you.

If your everyday is consumed with talking negatively about others, judging others, running around taking pictures of celebrities because your ego has complete control over you to hide your fears, then you will have the opportunity to experience this first hand.

All right, getting back to the two sides of my coin. Eventually this manifestation of every thought subsided. Imagine if everything you desired automatically appeared before your very eyes. Pretty damned awesome if you ask me! This is where we came from and this is where we are going. Soon if you are ready!

At this very moment I am able to manifest on a daily basis but it is nothing like it was during earlier times in my life. I feel somewhat disappointed as I believe that I was called and couldn't handle it and wasn't chosen to stay. As I am aware that my level of consciousness is higher than most, I am also aware that it has been lowered and I will have to work at raising it.

The other side of the coin is, I agreed to go through this prior to this incarnation so I could write this book and inform others as to what is coming around the corner soon. With this book, I want to help those who might be experiencing ascension now and those who will. I have always considered myself a very good leader and the toughest man I know. If you ask my peers about my leadership qualities, you will receive the same answer, this I know. But this isn't an easy process and can be very terrifying.

Experiencing these things that are out of this world will bring any man to his knees. You have heard it from the horse's mouth and hopefully this might alleviate some of the misperceptions that you might have heard about me.

I do not believe everyone will experience what I went through, as my purpose is different. Some refer to the very difficult time of tribulation as the Dark Night of the Soul; I told you earlier that I refer to my own experiences this way. This is a lengthy and profound absence of light and hope. There is much to learn from this experience and if you do go through it your job will be to convey it regardless of the naysayer. Jesus said, "Father, forgive them; for they know not what they do."[56] If only everyone knew what lies on the other side of the veil.

Be prepared for your calling and if you are full of love and devotion for others at that time, please tell us how heaven on earth is!

Conclusion

———————————— • ————————————

S O NOW YOU HAVE A TASTE OF WHAT my world has become.
Maybe it's what you expected after reading about me in a blog
or hearing one of my interviews. Or maybe it's not and you realize
that there are some really interesting things that impact your world.
Things you don't understand but want to open up to and learn
more about.

If it's the last part, then I've achieved my goal. The real purpose
of this book is to give you information that will allow you to be
aware of the powers that we all are capable of. Powers that for the
most part, have been dormant for a long time.

It is time for us to awaken and we are. I do not believe everyone
is ready for this awakening, though. No matter how connected we
all are, our spiritual growth is measured on an individual basis.
Piercing the veil is a personal endeavor that can only happen by and
through you and no one else. It is your soul, your life and your

destiny on your time. The only difference now from any other point in history is we are getting much needed help for this enlightenment and transformation to take place.

If this book flies and people start to awaken I will probably be led to write another book. Next time around I will take up some other so-called myths or mysteries such as controlling the weather around you. This is a wonderful phenomenon that can be realized and manifested in your conscious reality. If I haven't said it enough before, I'll say it again here. We are in control of everything in our realities and we just have to figure out where we hid the keys to unlock this mystery.

I've told you that the process of ascension isn't always an easy one. At its worst, its effects can seem impossible to take. Through much prayer, meditating and soul searching, I was able to get through this without being harmed. I was able to manifest quite a few trips to the pokey though. I mentioned earlier about four people who I read about in a book by the late author Lynn Grabhorn,[57] who she said couldn't physically and mentally handle this process and committed suicide. I personally experienced great difficulty, although not to that extent, and was fortunately led to her book at the end of this bizarre moment in my life. I wasn't quite sure at the time what was happening, but felt a little relieved after reading the exact experience from someone else.

But this is a pretty cool story, regardless of all that happened and how difficult it sometimes was for me. I hope there is enough information in this book to — at least — get you to be aware of a world that most of us don't even know exists and to comprehend that we are the ones creating it moment by moment.

If I have been redundant concerning certain things in this book it's because I meant to be. We, for whatever reason, are a species that requires repetition and redundancy to learn things correctly. I am just trying to inform you of the magic that awaits you. All of you doubting Thomas's keep your derogatory comments to yourselves. I already know your weaknesses, show me your strengths! This is an opportunity to expand your mind and to start using your divinity to experience all of it. Let's get you acclimated to what is happening first, and then gradually start feeding you the meat.

Start with taking some time and figure out who you are - who you REALLY are. Once you do, I guarantee you will stop judging others. That change in and of itself will change the world we collectively live in. Think about it, out of all the bizarre stories in this book, living in a world where nobody judges anyone else seems the most bizarre.

When Noah was building his boat, do you think people walked by and said, "I wonder where in the hell this guy is getting his information?" Do you ever think it crossed his mind that what he was doing probably looked silly to almost everyone else?

I've done what I have been asked to do.

It's really easy to believe. Just try it!

Endnotes

————————— • —————————

[1] Evin. *A 12-Dimensional Overview.* Retrieved 4/2007. http://www.life-enthusiast.com/news/s_ascension.htm

[2] Bishop, Karen. *The Ascension Primer: Life in the Higher Realms Series, Book One,* (Bangor: Booklocker.com, 2006). See also, <http://www.whatsuponplanetearth.com>

[3] See, Crystal, Ellie; 1995-2007, http://www.crystalinks.com/gridmetaphysics.html; http://www.crystalinks.com/grid.html

[4] Karen Bishop, www.whatsuponplanetearth.com <http://www.namastecafe.com/edu/symptoms.htm>

[5] See, *Descartes and the Pineal Gland* Stanford Encyclopedia of Philosophy, October 9, 2006; http://plato.stanford.edu/entries/pineal-gland/#2

[6] Crystal, Ellie, 1995-2007 <http://www.crystalinks.com/thirdeyepineal.html >

[7] Crystal, Ellie, 1995-2007 <http://www.crystalinks.com/thirdeyepineal.html>

[8] *Supernova Blast Begins Taking Shape.* January 14, 1997, http://hubblesite.org/newscenter/archive/releases/1997

[9] Donahue, Bill, 2007, The Pineal Gland of the Brain, http://

www.hiddenmeanings.com/cosmos.html,, Reprinted with Permission

[10] Donahue, Bill, 2007, Think About these Things / The Pineal Gland of the Brain, http://www.hiddenmeanings.com/think.html, Reprinted with Permission

[11] Donahue, Bill, 2007, Think About These Things / Jacob's Wrestling Match, http://www. Hiddenmeanings.com/think.html. Reprinted with Permission

[12] Crystal, Ellie; 1995-2007 "Kundalini Energy," <http://www.crystalinks.com/kundalini.htm>

[13] Crystal, Ellie; 1995-2007 "Kundalini Energy" <http://www.crystalinks.com/kundalini.htm>

[14] Donahue, Bill; 2007 "The Serpent:, http://www.hiddenmeanings.com/think.html; Reprinted with Permission

[15] Melchizedek, Drunvalo, *The Ancient Secret of the Flower of Life, Volume 2* (Light Technology Publications, 1999), 309; See also, *MerKaBa, A Vehicle of Ascension* 2006 <http://www.spiritofmaat.com/archive/sep2/merkaba.htm>

[16] *The Ancient Secret of the Flower of Life*, Drunvalo Melchizedek, Light Technology Publications, April 1999

[17] "DNA" *The American Heritage® Science Dictionary*. Houghton Mifflin Company. 09 Jul. 2007. <Dictionary.com http://dictionary.reference.com/browse/DNA>.

[18] Thorpe-Clark, Susanna , July 2007 <http://www.life-enthusiast.com/news/s_ascension.htm>

[19] Crystal, Ellie, *Encoded Digital Messages* 1995-2007, <http://www.crystalinks.com/11.11.html>

[20] Crystal, Ellie, *Encoded Digital Messages* 1995-2007, <http://www.crystalinks.com/11.11.html>

[21] Crystal, Ellie, *Encoded Digital Messages* 1995-2007, <http://www.crystalinks.com/11.11.html>

[22] September11news.com, 2001-2003, <http://www.september11news.com/Mysteries2.htm >

[23] *The Exorcist*, Directed by William Friedkin, Warner Brothers Pictures, 1973

[24] Watson, Lyall, Ph.D. *Lifetide* (London: Hodder & Stoughton Ltd., 1979)

[25] Keyes, Ken, Jr. *The Hundredth Monkey.* (Camarillo, CA: Devorss & Co., 2nd Ed. June 2004; as reprinted, 2000-2005). See also, http://www.lightshift.com/Inspiration/monkey.html

[26] *Multiplicity*, Directed by Harold Ramis, Columbia Pictures Corporation, 1996

[27] Solsbury Hill, Peter Gabriel, 1990; Album: "Shaking The Tree: Sixteen Golden Greats"

[28] Sacred geometry. *Wikipedia, The Free Encyclopedia.* 20 Jul 2007, 09:41 UTC. Wikimedia Foundation, Inc. 23 Jul 2007 <http://www. wikipedia.org/Sacred_geometry5>.

[29] *The Matrix*, Directed by Andy Wachowski and Larry Wachowski, Groucho II Film Partnership, 1999

[30] *The Philadelphia Experiment*, Directed by Stewart Raffill, Cinema Group Ventures, 1984 .

[31] U.S. Department of the Navy; Naval Historical Center Home Page; November 18, 2000, <http://www.history.navy.mil/faqs/faq21-1.htm>

[32] Nee, Watchman, *Spiritual Man, Volume 2*, (Richmond, VA: Christian Fellowship Publishers, 1968), 56

[33] Nee, Watchman, *Spiritual Man, Volume 2*, 56

[34] Nee, Watchman, *Spiritual Man, Volume 2*, 56

[35] Job 2:6. "And the Lord said to Satan, "Behold, he is in your power; only spare his life." (Revised Standard Version)

[36] Ephesians 2: 1-2. "And you he made alive, when you were dead through the trespasses and sins in which you once walked, following the course of this world, following the prince of the power of the air, the spirit that is now at work in the sons of disobedience. (Revised Standard Version)

[37] "Bewitched." Ashmont Productions, 1964-1972

[38]: Matthew 18:12-14. "What do you think? If a man has a hundred sheep, and one of them has gone astray, does he not leave the ninety-nine on the hills and go in search of the one that went astray? And if he finds it, truly, I say to you,

he rejoices over it more than over the ninety-nine that never went astray."
(RSV) See also, Luke 15:2-7

[39] John 14:2 "In my Father's house are many mansions: if it were not so, I
would have told you. I go to prepare a place for you." (King James Version)

[40] See, for example, <http://www.december212012.com>

[41] See for example, "Decoding The Past, Doomsday 2012: The End of Days"
The History Channel. 2006 <http://www.history.com>

[42] *WAFB Special Report, The End of Time*, May 2, 2007, <http://
www.december212012.com/articles/news/10.htm>

[43] Weinhold, Janae, *2012: Ascension, Rebirth and the Dimensional Shift.* 6 June
2007 <http://weinholds.org/2012_home.asp>

[44] Matthew 22:14 "For many are called, but few are chosen." (Revised Standard
Version)

[45] Matthew 26:52 "Then Jesus said to him, "Put your sword back into its place;
for all who take the sword will perish by the sword." (Revised Standard
Version)

[46] John 14:12 "Truly, truly I say to you, he who believes in me will also do the
works that I do; and greater works than these will he do, because I go to the
Father." (Revised Standard Version)

[47] Melchizedek, The Ancient Secret of the Flower of Life, 438-439

[48] Melchizedek, The Ancient Secret of the Flower of Life, 438-439

[49] Matthew 25:13 "(Revised Standard Version)

[50] Luke 23:34 (Revised Standard Version)

[51] Grabhorn, Lynn *Dear God! What's Happening to Us?: Halting Eons of
Manipulation* (Charlottesville: Hampton Roads Publishing Company, 2003)